JOSIAH

JOSIAH

ONE FAMILY'S JOURNEY OF BEING BROKEN TOGETHER

MARIA KOUTS

AWAKEN ✿ VILLAGE

PRESS

This is a work of nonfiction. Any resemblance to persons living or dead should be plainly apparent to them and those who know them, especially if the author has been kind enough to have provided their real names. All events described herein are all true from the author's perspective.

The content of this book is for general instruction only. Each person's physical, emotional, and spiritual condition is unique. The instruction in this book is not intended to replace or interrupt the reader's relationship with a counselor, physician, or other mental health professional.

Printed in the United States of America.

Editing by Amanda Johnson
Cover and interior design by Tim Murray

ISBN 978-1-7344265-0-2 (paperback)
ISBN 978-1-7344265-1-9 (ebook)
Library of Congress Control Number: 2019920760
Published by Awaken Village Press

www.awakenvillagepress.com

I wish to dedicate this book to my family; they are the real MVP. This work is "our" work, not just mine. My husband, Jason, whose love and resolve is unwavering, has given me the liberty to write every ugly detail of our lives because he has the same heart as I do. We want to use our story to help others who may have been naively exposed to the world of drugs. My daughter, Montana, whose deep affection for me is fierce and protective and, even though she is a private person, supports me a hundred percent and understands why I have to write our story. My younger son, Austin, is my rock. He stands beside me, unwavering in his devotion and respect for me. We are a cohesive unit that embodies the concept of "together, we are strong."

Together, we will continue to turn the pages of our beloved Josiah's book of life. He died way too early but will live on through us.

"REPEATED CYCLES OF PAIN"

I'm fine, I say over and over
Push you away, afraid you'll get closer
Isolate emotions is what I do
Cause you'd hurt me deeply, if you knew
Denial has become my very best friend
Can't admit my shame for it may rend
I give up hope, filled with despair
Bury it deeper, no one will care
Plaster.   On.   A big wide smile
No one will see my emotional pile
It goes down deep, no one can see
God I feel broken, I wanna be free
In this life I'm the victim, hurry and hide
I gotta feel numb again

— Maria Kouts

CONTENTS

Introduction

WE LIVE IN GNARLY TIMES. It can be so easy to sit around and be the victim, talking about how unfair life is. We can grow bitter and cynical and lay down and not fight, or we can choose to become well-equipped and educate ourselves and live with purpose.

Drugs are an epidemic. However, many people think it will never touch their own. I am a mom who is completely transparent with my children. I told them all my failures in an attempt to educate them so they would be armed to make better decisions. My kids were my life! My whole world was wrapped up in being a good mom. The thought of one of my kids ever touching drugs never once crossed my mind.

The number of families affected by drugs is growing exponentially. Many families are swimming in a sea of pain and anger, disbelief, and a lack of knowledge. Many parents feel completely alone and unable to save their loved ones. We live in a world full of emotionally broken, crippled, wounded people—people who run away from God because of their brokenness and shame; people who live in repeated cycles of pain and immaturity. This is where my journey began: the acknowledgment of my crippled, arrested emotions.

When our emotions get stuffed down and hidden, they become arrested and, just like an iceberg, only ten percent of our reality is above water. The other ninety percent manifests itself in many kinds of addictions. Families affected by drugs have the propensity to hide their lives and feelings for fear of rejection and severe ridicule. This is a breeding ground for addiction.

This book is intended to reach below the surface into your most vulnerable areas and the parts that you have kept hidden away from a cruel, judgmental world. My prayer is that this book will give you the courage to pull out all the hidden things in your life because anything hidden never heals.

If you don't heal what is buried inside of you, it transfers onto the ones you love the most. Our lives are singing a song and its lyrics are read most frequently by our children. We pass down belief systems and perspectives and ways of coping. My choice of coping was hiding all my feelings and emotions from my conscious awareness, and it resulted in emotional numbness. My husband coped by letting his feelings and emotions run wild, which came out in aggression and anger. Anger and shame then joined together to produce a hybrid of bitterness and resentment. This was in the formidable years of child-rearing. We set the stage and prepared the fertile ground for dysfunction to be planted.

The good news is that it's never too late.

The message in this book is intended to inspire, educate, strengthen, and comfort you. The learning process I had to go through was difficult. The unlearning of the ways of the world in which I lived was the hardest part. Writing it all down was brutal; expression deepens impression. Getting inside my deepest suffering and despair required me to become vulnerable and transparent and, most of all, trusting. As often as I despaired, God also strengthened me more and more.

I want to use my life to share the message God gave me. I believe I was made for "such a time as this," when our world is experiencing the worst drug epidemic of all time. Mine is a personal story of loss and tragedy, but, as with mine, it never needs to end there. There is hope, and I pray that you will find it in the pages of this book.

If you allow this book to speak to your life and circumstances, it has the potential to help you navigate the ugliness of addiction along with the dysfunction deep within your soul. Many parents have a hard time accepting their responsibility in the addiction and simultaneously understanding that the addict makes his or her own decision to use drugs. It's a fine line to walk and one that is necessary to stay on in order to be healthy. Accept your part in the dysfunction while, at the same time, unlearning your unhealthy way of doing things that contribute to the dysfunction. When you are healthy as a parent, you have a much greater chance in helping your addict.

The world statistic of sobriety in an intravenous heroin user is a 1% success rate. That is a staggering statistic. However, through Christ all things are possible. I attend church with loads of sober intravenous heroin users—some with up to twenty years of sobriety. I believe with my whole heart that we should not accept the statistics. Instead, we are called to rise up and fight and take our nation back from these drugs. We are called to learn a healthy way to deal with our demons and unlearn all the toxic ways. It isn't easy to admit failure, and it's even harder to unlearn what we think is truth our entire lives, but we must do it anyway. When we go through the unlearning process, it always leads to the promise!

Understand you have what it takes through Christ to take this head-on. I pray as you read this book that the Holy Spirit will get down deep to the hidden places and give you the strength and courage to expose those broken places. Instead of running away and hiding from God, you run straight into His arms. You go first! Your loved ones will see the change, and it will help give them the tenacity and spirit to also heal what is hidden.

We can all be a "beacon of light" to those who are

hurting around us. Allow the sanctification process to begin inside of you and leave the outcome to God, the One who can heal us completely. He will never turn His back on you! In fact, He is your shield as you navigate through the minefield. Stay attached to the source of life, and He will continue to nourish, transform, feed, change, and restore you. Let your Shepherd attend to your wounds and brokenness; He is the only one able. He is your safe place. Go to Him, and He will give you your life back. He will bless you beyond measure and give you what you need to slay every giant. He is your anchor in the fiercest of storms.

If you or your family has been affected by the drug epidemic, you are not alone. Be encouraged in the Lord.

Blessings,

Maria Kouts

CHAPTER 1
Pride and Joy

STARTLED OUT OF A DEEP SLEEP, disoriented and foggy, I reach for my cell phone ringing from the bedside table. "Hello?" I speak in a quiet, raspy voice. "This is Mount Graham Community Hospital calling on behalf of Josiah Kouts. Is this his mom?" I sit up alert and glance over at the clock. Midnight. "Yes, this is Ma..." The man cut me off, "Your son has overdosed. They're working on him, but he's been without oxygen for four to five minutes now, and it doesn't look good." His voice grows muted as I attempt to process what he said. My mind is reeling. A wave of nausea and panic hit my soul as I ask him, "What doesn't look good?" Obviously pressed, he tells me to get there as quickly as I can.

I hang up the phone. My husband, Jason, now sitting up in bed. I relay the situation as best I can, and we throw on clothes and head out the door. I shiver as I step outside, the crisp midnight air biting my skin, my breath rolling out in a fog of condensation. I am breathing heavily, fear gripping my heart. The drive to the hospital, only minutes away, seems to last an eternity.

> "But you, O Lord, are a shield
> around me, my glory, the one
> who lifts my head high."
> — *Psalm* 3:3

I WAS TWO WEEKS OVERDUE and ready to get this baby out of me. The doctor decided to induce labor, hooking me up to an IV and feeding my veins Pitocin. I walked the halls for several hours until the pain was too extreme to stand. It was 1992 in the small city of Safford, Arizona. The professionals didn't offer an epidural. I had to deliver the old-fashioned way: hard and long. I checked into the hospital at seven in the morning for a labor that would take all day, finally resulting in a ten-centimeter dilation. By evening, I was ready to push. After a couple hours of pushing, my body and unborn baby were in distress. The doctor knew it was time for an emergency C-section.

I was an eighteen-year-old baby having a baby. I desperately wanted the pain to end, swearing I'd never do this again. I was screaming in pain as Jason held my hand and they rolled me to the operating room. As it was an emergency, they wouldn't let him inside the room. I was shaking uncontrollably, my body reacting to the stress and narcotics. "Be still," the doctor instructed. He had to insert the needle into my back perfectly; it was imperative I didn't move. I remember the moment the medicine entered my body, all the pain subsiding. My anesthesiologist kindly stroked my face, assuring me everything was going to be okay. The room was cold and bright. All I could see was the blue sheet that stretched from my chest straight up in the air, my lower extremities hidden from view. Waves of nausea hit me, which the doctor told me was normal. And then, a cry! My eight-pound-fourteen-ounce baby boy was breathing and healthy and huge. That's the last thing I remember.

I woke up in recovery, unable to control my shaking. As I opened my eyes, there he was beside me, warm in an incubator. He was wide awake, his big round eyes fully open and staring straight at me. I couldn't move and began to cry. A nurse came quickly to explain my numbness and shaking, which were a result of the epidural and anesthesia. Seeing Josiah for the first time, my heart was overflowing. Until that moment, I hadn't known real love.

Josiah was a happy baby. He lit up around people, but all he really wanted was his mama. He knew his animal sounds, could count to five, and was potty-trained, all before he was a year old. We called him "Baby Einstein" and marveled at his clever, brainy, brilliant self. I was overprotective and didn't want anyone babysitting him. He was my first baby, my first love, my bouncing bundle of life. I didn't want a single person having an opinion or say in his little life. I had a picture in my mind of what love looked like and how love was to be carried out, and I was convinced that I was fully capable; no one's help was needed.

When Josiah was two, I had another baby. Montana was the polar opposite of Josiah, crying from the start. All my attention went to my new baby, especially when all she did was cry. Josiah wanted to hold her and bounce her and talk to her, even when she was screaming. He was the proverbial older brother, running to get me diapers or a towel, answering the door, and entertaining his baby sister. His eyes danced with anticipation of what he could help with next. Two years after Montana's arrival, our youngest child, Austin, was born. He was a mini Jason and has been the joy of my heart from day one.

For the first fourteen years of Josiah's life, Jason and I were dirt poor. We'd often have to go to Jason's mom's house to raid her pantry for food. Jason worked seemingly nonstop to support us, putting in forty hours at his dad's family business. Still, it wasn't enough to pay rent, so he'd walk door to door around town asking if he could mow the lawn or trim trees. He took any side work he could find, working sunup to sundown, seven days a week. It allowed us to make rent most months. Jason didn't want me working, which I now understand was a true blessing, affording me the luxury of being a full-time mom, not relying on a babysitter to raise our kids. He wanted me to raise them while he made our living.

My identity as a mom was born.

My three little ones had no idea we were poor. It wasn't a conscious reality in our family. Jason worked hard and paid the bills, but we lived paycheck to paycheck. I had been raised this way, so for me, it was normal, and I raised our kids to not know any different. We lived happily in a travel trailer for a six-month stint, our lives adventurous and joyful, inspired by our firstborn, our pride and joy.

Jason and I met when we were in high school. One week after I graduated high school, Jason and I got married. I was ready to party hard; Jason hated every minute of it. A couple years after having Josiah, our marriage hit a rough patch. We were fighting like cats and dogs. Both the babies of our respective families, we each desired to have things "our way." Jason was an ambitious workaholic; I was a lonely twenty-year-old with a wild streak and lots of time on my hands. When Jason got home from work he would play video games until time for bed. The cycle would continue each day, and I was miserable. I picked many fights just to get him to pay attention to me, although the end result was always the same—more withdrawal and isolation. I didn't know what a healthy marriage looked like, but I was sure it was nothing like what we were living. I was mad and hurt. Jason was withdrawn and aloof. The combination was combustible at best. My marriage was in shambles, and I had no one to talk to other than "religious" people who told me what a sinner I was. My conversations with Jason were painful and toxic.

It was 1994, I had two babies and was a twenty-one-year-old "work widow." I developed a friendship with a man who became my best friend and the only person I could talk to about the problems I was having in my marriage. I quickly became emotionally attached to him. He made all the time in the world for me. We would console one another and talk through our problems together. We became intimate and shattered Jason's whole world.

On one occasion, after much hurt and dysfunction, things escalated. I was completely done. Jason knew it. He went into our closet where we had a 9mm pistol, shutting and locking the door behind him. He said he was done living.

The ring of the round firing forced time to stand still for what seemed like forever. His body hit the wall and slid down.... Silence. I came to my senses, realizing what had happened, and began pounding on the door, screaming his name. "JASON, JASON, JASON, ANSWER ME, OH MY GOD, JASON!" We don't realize the strength we have until a moment like that—I kicked in the door with my heart pounding, mind racing, and adrenaline pumping.

There he stood, totally unscathed. He had shot the

gun and pretended he shot himself to see if I was truly done with our marriage or if there was a shred of hope or love left in me. Suddenly, I was swinging my fists as hard as I could, aiming for every part of his body. We both ended up on the floor of the closet, crying and wondering what was happening to us. Despite the terror and anger I felt, there was still a sliver of love that remained.

During all this, Josiah was hiding under my bed crying while Montana stayed asleep in her room. I went to lie beside Josiah and asked him if he was okay. What he told me that day is forever etched in my mind. "Aunty L," he began, referring to my sister, "told me that every time you and dad fight, I can pray and Jesus will come and help you. I was praying." My little man's words broke something inside me; a crack formed in my walls. I knew Jesus had heard that cry for help. I didn't know a way his daddy and I would make our marriage work at that point, but I knew that his little prayer was being answered.

Josiah would live up to his Biblical name—Jehovah has healed, and it all began on that day.

Our children experienced and lived through some pretty severe fights and watched as Jason and I found our way through circumstances that should have ruined us. Hurt lingered in our marriage for many formative years in a child's life.

Josiah's bright little personality shifted for a couple years. He became quiet and sad; meanwhile, Montana did nothing but cry. Austin was a newborn baby and, luckily, has no recollection of those days. I was naive at the time, not realizing how my behavior was causing my children to suffer. Nor did I comprehend the gravity of the emotions they were dealing with. Trauma at a young age convolutes what is normal and healthy.

Though Jason and I struggled in our relationship, we both remained committed to healing it. Finally, life began to grow within our marriage once again. We had conversations and eventually became best friends again. Jason chose to limit his workday to eight hours and come home. We finally had a family unit. Jason looked at me with such love. It was the happiest time of my life. Our kids flourished. After years of struggling financially, Jason had a developer approach him and ask if he'd like to build houses for him. The market was good, and many people were building and buying homes. It was our big break! His company was prospering. God had completely transformed all of us, giving us a first-hand experience of "He gives beauty for ashes."

Throughout grade school and high school, Josiah had many nicknames, among them "preacher kid" because he saw people—really saw them—and was easily moved to compassion. He was a shining star, a straight-A student, the class clown, and the teacher's pet. He was extremely smart without having to try too hard at school. It came very naturally to him. He made friends easily and surrounded himself with people day in and day out. Josiah, more than anyone else in our family, had always thrived on and gained energy from other people. He had a way of connecting with others. In his presence, they felt loved and valued. He spent his time and energy making life an adventure, and others naturally wanted to take part.

Smart, quick-witted, and fearless, he was the mastermind of new ideas and their detailed implementation. He orchestrated clubs around whatever particular interests he had at the time. He had a bicycle club, a fort club, a car club, a gamers' club, just to name a few. He was the oldest child and knew how to run the show. Our house was filled with the energy and excitement of all the neighborhood kids hanging out at our house on a constant basis. He lit up the room with his dazzling smile and gregarious personality. He loved life and lived it fast-paced and "in the moment"—until drug addiction.

Like Jason, Josiah didn't have a lazy bone in his body, and, like me, he loved making things an adventure. He never slowed down. He was brave and loved living on the edge, never afraid of heights or challenges. In fact, he loved anything that made his heart skip a beat. Given both Jason and I are adventurous to the core, jumping on new, exciting exploits, we loved this about Josiah.

One year, he gained an interest in bicycle ramps, and Jason built him one that was five feet tall. It drew in people who loved skateboards, bicycles, and scooters. Kids from all over the valley would come to our house, Josiah always the front and center of attention. He was the kind of kid who got along with everyone, never having a true enemy. Kids would do the hurtful things that kids do, teasing or insulting him, but he took it in stride, like water off a duck's back, quick to forgive. From the earliest age, Josiah bounced back from all kinds of hardship to regain his sparkly personality. It was one of his greatest assets. He'd fall down, but he always got back up again.

The years of adolescence are often tough. Middle school proved to be a daunting challenge with lots of heartache for Montana and Austin. Josiah faced all the same pressures but didn't seem to struggle. He breezed through despite mean kids, even creating friends out of haters. He didn't have to be smarter, better, or more athletic. He always seemed secure in who he was and what he possessed. He lived a happy life and made bad situations good with his dynamic personality and willingness to go the extra mile to make peace.

Tiny in stature until after graduation, he wasn't deterred from playing all kinds of sports. He lived like he was a giant and had a heart to match. He made the junior high basketball team with fourteen teammates—all big guys. Collectively, the team was rock solid, winning a majority of their games. Josiah would sit and cheer for his team the entire game, getting some playing time in the final few minutes. He'd get in the game for the last minute or two and play with all that he had.

It was part of his character to be "all in" with whatever he was involved in. He didn't even have to love it; he was just happy to be a part of something. He seemed just as happy sitting on the bench as he was on the floor playing. He embodied team spirit, a team player who was loved by all his teammates.

Basketball was never Josiah's love; it was his mama's, and he went along with what I wanted for him. A basketball player myself, I loved the game and thought all my kids would have the same love. I was doing what I thought every "good" mother did, expressing my love for my children by being the best mother I could be. I never even asked him if he wanted to play basketball, and he never argued when I'd sign him up. He was just that kind of kid, easygoing and congenial. He rolled with life. Whether he liked it or not, he made the best of anything he participated in.

Josiah obeyed the rules and lived life through a lens that viewed each day as full of distinct possibilities to challenge him and keep him moving forward. A new day was a chance to make more friends and fun memories, to explore and create, learn and grow. School, friends, sports, family, and church were Josiah's blank canvases as he painted his masterpiece daily.

People would often tell me something I still hear today—teenage years are a tough challenge. I didn't experience that with my kids. Their teenage years, in fact, were my favorite ones of all. I was busy but so fulfilled. I loved my life and felt blessed beyond measure with amazing kids. I felt like I was living the American dream. That's not to say I didn't get a phone call or two from high school teachers. One day, I got a call from the school. I answered, expecting to hear Montana's or Josiah's voice. Instead, it was Josiah's teacher on the phone. She'd called to tell me something Josiah had done in class, which I immediately suspected would be along the lines of "sticking up for the underdog" or "going above and beyond."

"Mrs. Kouts," she began, "today in class, Josiah had his hands under his desk." Her voice began to get choked up and she struggled to finish. "Is everything okay?" I asked. She attempted to compose herself, speaking with a shaky voice. "I asked him what he was doing, and he told me he was scratching his...." "His what?" I said. "His nuts!" she blurted, "He said he was scratching his nuts!"

I burst out laughing. She continued as if deaf to my laughter, "Mrs. Kouts, I don't know what you encourage in your home, but it's inappropriate to say things like that in class!" After gaining my composure, I explained that I had trained my children to be honest. She had asked him what he was doing, and he told her the truth. My reaction was so upsetting to her that she hung up on me. Don't ask my kids if you don't want the truth!

When he turned sixteen, Josiah got into gaming, playing video games for hours at a time. I am not sure why I permitted him to check out of the real world and into a fake one in such a way. I didn't realize it at the time, but it was much like how Jason and I would check out in the early days of our marriage to avoid the pain and anger we felt. Four months into my pregnancy with Josiah, I stopped smoking and drinking, but I still wanted to go to parties. Everything seemed like forbidden fruit, and I couldn't stand to miss out anymore. Jason put his foot down and insisted we were done with partying. Meanwhile, I noticed when he got home after working long hours, he'd play video games until bedtime.

I convinced myself Josiah was simply competitive and wanted to be the best and that he got a sense of that from gaming. I wish I would have had more insight at the time. He'd go hours without eating or drinking. What I now understand to be early signs of addiction, often bred out of not knowing how to deal with or express the pain going on within, I was unaware of then.

At the age of seventeen, Josiah started going to parties on the weekends. He was the designated driver and the entertainment for his friends. He loved the girls, cozying up to them while his buddies partied. But it wasn't long before he began drinking. I first found out at Montana's sweet sixteen birthday party.

I had enlisted the help of my closest friends, my nieces, and their husbands to monitor and supervise the kids at my house during the birthday festivities. It was a giant party, and before I knew it, all the adult supervisors were drunk and dancing and doling out the alcohol. Josiah was also a willing recipient and drank until he was drunk.

The next year, we had a graduation party for Josiah. Again, many kids snuck alcohol and drank. I didn't see it as anything serious, just kids being kids. I had educated my kids on alcohol and drinking and driving and felt pretty safe they wouldn't abuse it. His experiences with alcohol, to my knowledge, were few and far between until graduation.

In my mind, drinking alcohol was permissible to anyone who did it legally. My wishes for my children would have been to do things according to the law and not the pressures of others. That said, I was never a stickler regarding my now-adult kids having alcohol. I didn't want alcohol to be the forbidden fruit they had to get their hands on at any cost like it had been for me.

My senior year was my first time getting drunk. My mom and dad had to make a trip to Tucson, and I went to hang out with an older friend. I drank a fifth of rum. By myself. I had never been educated on the effects or dangers of alcohol, always getting the black-and-white "don't touch alcohol" speech. It panned out to be quite ineffective. I should have died that day.

I would never buy my children alcohol illegally but didn't make a big fuss when they'd tell me they drank some. I never wanted my kids to feel they had to hide things from me. In fact, I told them to call me and tell me—I wouldn't be mad—if they ever messed up and got into any trouble. From the time they were little, I'd been educating them on drinking and driving and the damage it could do. It would be better for them to call me than get behind the wheel and possibly hurt themselves or another human being.

Josiah graduated in May of 2011 and was off to college by August. He worked for his dad over the summer after not having worked for him for many years. Jason had Josiah on roofs throwing shingles from the age of two, thinking he'd hand the business down to his firstborn. But that wasn't who Josiah was. Josiah believed in working smarter, not harder. Going into high school, he had worked various jobs around town. A brainy kid, he knew he could make money by using his smarts and didn't hesitate to tell his dad how much construction sucked. It devastated Jason, who always believed he would raise his boys the way his dad had raised him—to take over the family business.

Jason is one of the most upstanding guys I know. He is a provider by nature and knew he could train his sons in his business and subsequently provide for them long-term. His father was hardworking and carried over that quality in his son's upbringing. Jason's mom raised the kids while his dad worked to provide everything the family needed, a tradition that Jason continued in his own parenting, which wasn't extremely "hands on."

Work was his place of refuge, a place to go when life hurt him or kicked him down. Jason's entire identity has been built upon his ability to create with construction. A workaholic with his construction business the object of his obsession, Jason wanted his older son to be the heir of his trade. When Josiah didn't want any part in his work, Jason took it as a direct rejection of who he was as a person.

Even though construction and manual labor weren't his strong suit, that summer, Josiah once again worked for Jason, playing hard in the evenings and weekends with his "new toy," whether a bike or scooter, a car or hot wheel, a new video game; he used the money he earned to take part in the recreation of his choice.

In those years, addiction was nowhere in my frame of reference.

CHAPTER 2
Numbing Out

HAVING GRADUATED HIGH SCHOOL with honors, ready to start college life, Josiah was full of ambition for his future. Jason and I had procured for him an apartment and furniture, and off we went to move our son to his new life in the big city.

I went shopping, stocking his apartment with food, toiletries, and cleaning supplies. His apartment was in the heart of Mesa, walking distance to Mesa Community College and about twenty minutes from Phoenix. He called me after school on the first and second days, telling me he'd found his classes and was loving it there. I was elated—my firstborn had graduated from high school and was off to college.

As a mom, I felt like I'd accomplished exactly what I set out for. Every mom wants to know her children will be prepared to live on their own, able to provide for themselves and be self-sufficient when they reach adulthood. At some point, mama eagle gently pushes them over the edge of the nest to figure out the strength of their own wings and fly alone. I wanted my adult children to be happy and live lives that were guided and shaped by a loving mom who took great pleasure and thoughtful measures in having spent their first eighteen years beside them. The day they move out is the day I get to watch what all those years of parenting have taught them...or so I thought.

Josiah had been at college for a couple of months when I got a disturbing phone call. One of Montana's friends had been to the city and seen Josiah over the weekend. She told Montana he was ninety pounds and strung out on drugs, that he was in trouble and I needed to come get him straight away. I was completely caught off guard. Josiah on drugs? Drugs were for streetwalkers, for messed up families led by imprisoned fathers and strung-out mothers. Drugs would never affect my children.

With this predetermined picture of what kind of people did drugs, my mind was certain my kids would never be one of them. I was so stuck in my judgmental, small-minded thinking, it had never even occurred to me to educate my kids on drugs' effects. The admission makes me sick. At the time, I thought of pot smokers as the low-life, lazy Americans who check out on life and leave it to the diligent working class to support them.

I didn't see a connection between the ways in which our family already had plenty of experience checking out—video games, work, shopping—and drug use. In my mind, drugs were in a class of their own; nothing else could compare. It's since become clearer that the labels and judgments that we place on people are precisely what leads to the alienation that can so easily perpetuate addiction.

Jason and I loaded into my car and headed for the city. I spent the drive to Mesa thinking how sadly mistaken this friend had been about Josiah. It was Josiah—my greatest accomplishment, the kid I never exchanged harsh words with. A good boy, a mama's boy, my pride and joy. My self-conception as his mother and my perception of who he was as a human being were all tied together in my neat little box called "my life." There would be no way to accept that something like this could happen in "my life." This rumor was just par for the course for someone like Josiah, who had it all and could bounce back from anything.

Jason and I climbed the stairs, rounding the corner to land on his doorstep. We happily gave a little knock knock. "Josiah, it's mom and dad. You in there?" I could hear a television inside, but there was no answer. I knocked again and tried to twist the doorknob, but it was locked. A young man answered the door and winced as the sunshine hit his face from outside. Inside, the apartment was pitch black. He was dressed only in shorts, his hair disheveled. It seemed as though we'd just woken him up. I asked the kid who he was and where Josiah was. He opened the door wide and said, "They're in the room."

We stepped inside. I was completely taken aback by what I saw. There was no table, no couch, nothing at all. The apartment was empty. I stormed by the young man and headed straight to Josiah's room, opening the door. Again, there was no furniture. Only two bodies—Josiah and his girlfriend—lying on the floor in near pitch black. I turned on the light and barely recognized my son as one of them.

I scooped up his emaciated frame in my arms. His beautiful face was covered in sores. I rocked his tiny body back and forth. "No, no, no, not my Siah." As the tears flowed, I told myself I had to be strong for my son. So I started with a pep talk. That was sure to save him. "Son, this was a crazy, silly mistake. We're putting you in the car and taking you home. I'm calling all your professors and telling them you need a week off. You're going to be okay, Josiah. I have no idea how this happened, but you're strong and capable. You just fell down, is all." As he became more responsive to me, I got up and started looking for something I could put his clothes in.

"Josiah..." I started. "Yeah, ma?" he mumbled. "Where's all your furniture?" He told me a crazy story that would become my first recollection of talking to an addict. He said that his buddy had to pay off a debt and then didn't have anywhere to live so Josiah let him move in. Josiah would give anyone the shirt off his back, and I found it plausible that he had given his furniture to "less fortunate" people to pay off his friend's debt. Although he admitted to having taken drugs, he wouldn't take actual responsibility, shifting all the blame onto others. We loaded him and his girlfriend into the car and headed back toward Safford. On our way home, I talked about everything going on in our lives: what Montana was up to, what Austin was dealing with at school, anything to avoid acknowledging the reality of my current experience.

I turned mid-sentence to look at Josiah and saw his head limply bobbing up and down, his eyes half-closed. "Josiah, what drug did you take?" "Heroin, ma," he answered. My head was swimming, my heart pounding as my chest began to tighten. "Heroin?" I asked myself, "Did he just say heroin? Like the men coming back from the Vietnam War strung out on heroin? Like the guys who stick needles in their arms? Heroin was a hardcore drug. It would certainly never touch my family!"

As I was contemplating what my son had just said, out of my mouth came, "We knew a guy who attended our church who'd inject himself with heroin, putting needles in his veins. A Vietnam vet. He had waist-long grey hair and a beard that went clear down to his chest. He always looked like death—a skeleton, devoid of spirit..." Josiah began to cry. He told me he wanted off, that if he'd ever known what it would do to him, he never would have tried it. One of his best friends growing up introduced it to him, needle and drug. He started off and ended up saying he just liked to party and have fun and that his desire to live on the edge simply went too far. I never thought that was the full story. But, for the time being, it was all I needed to hear. I didn't hesitate to believe him. Josiah loved and thrived off of challenges, so I set it in my mind that he would get home, rest, and be back to school in no time.

How naive I was.

We got home and neither he nor his girlfriend wanted to rest. They were out the door as soon as we arrived. I didn't worry, though. I figured he was safe at home. Of course, he wanted to see all his friends. Life would soon be back to normal.

They didn't come home that night. I called his phone several times, but I wasn't a reactionary mom, so I dismissed any thoughts of foul play. Jason, however, didn't sleep. He paced the floors and worried all night. I kept assuring him everything would be okay, that they'd just run into Josiah's friends and let time slip away. I thought maybe they'd fallen asleep watching a movie or played video games all night.

How naive I was.

They rolled in the next evening and told us they'd been at a friend's house and wanted to do some catching up. They hadn't brought phone chargers and their phones had died. I believed him hook, line, and sinker. Josiah was my honest kid, my good boy, who had never given me a day of trouble.

Complete denial was my first name. I didn't entertain a single thought that my son could be addicted to drugs. An addict son would mean I had completely failed as a parent.

When I finally permitted myself to realize what we were dealing with, I went straight into "saving him" mode. At the same time, because I was so naive, I thought it would be a quick fix and that all this would soon be behind us.

For the next week, Josiah remained isolated from the family. He stayed in his room, not even coming out to eat. I had to go to his room to force him to eat. He'd spend endless hours sitting there, scrolling on his phone. His head would droop over as if he was falling asleep, his eyes blinking slowly as if he couldn't quite open them. I constantly asked him why he was so tired, and he'd always say the same thing: "I can't sleep at night."

They had been at our house for a week, and he didn't seem to be improving. He was still all scabbed up. He didn't show any drive or spirit. I asked him if he was ready to go back to school, and he said he didn't plan to resume college at all that year. He said he needed a break. He couldn't take the pressure. I argued that he was strong and brilliant and had scholarships and a beautiful life in front of him. I was still stuck in the belief that addiction could only impact certain types of people. My unconscious judgment and shame blinded me from the truth.

Over time, I started to realize it wasn't only the

"lazy lowlifes" who get into drugs. Overachieving, high-performing people can just as easily succumb to them. But still, there remains a common thread: the labels we assign, whether "lowlife" or "pride and joy," become an identity people feel pressured to maintain at all costs.

I decided I'd get him some help on my own. He didn't fight with me. He didn't say anything at all, mindlessly scrolling through social media, day in and day out. I Googled around, collecting numbers that seemed like they might be able to support us. The first number I called told me Josiah himself would have to be the one to reach out for help. I dismissed that as an option, jumping right on the next one, and then the next one, and the next. I was such a novice to addiction and the whole world surrounding it. I believed I could just make a phone call and get everything I needed to make my son well again. I couldn't imagine the obstacles I'd face, or that I'd be unable to make calls on behalf of him. Josiah was sick; I wasn't. I felt fully capable of making calls and getting the answers I needed to help my son.

The last gentlemen I spoke to jolted me into reality. He asked me if Josiah was an intravenous heroin user. I had no idea what that meant. When I say I was naive, I mean it literally! I didn't know what I was asking him until the man explained, and even then I disbelieved Josiah would ever do drugs and especially not with a needle. After I confirmed that he indeed was an intravenous user, the man responded with, "Ma'am, I'm so sorry. Just know you're not alone. This is going to be a long journey."

The man asked me how long it had been since Josiah used. I told him I'd recently picked him up from Phoenix and what had happened since he got back home. The kind man, so gentle but straightforward, told me from my description of Josiah's behavior that he believed Josiah was currently high and had either brought the drug home with him or found more in Safford.

The weight of his words crushed my spirit. I cried, asking, pleading, "What can I do to save my son?" I assured him this was so unlike my Josiah, that he just needed me to help him get clean. Prior to this point, I'd never been around anyone who did drugs. I didn't know a single thing about them; I'd been so far removed from all of that. I didn't know any signs or symptoms of drug use. All I knew was I'd taken my amazing, smart, happy, thriving son to college, and he came back a lifeless skeleton with no smile, hiding away in his room.

Why had I never heard of anyone else in the Gila Valley who was going through this? I began hearing whispers of people whose children were addicted to drugs, but no one was willing to talk about it. I felt isolated and alone. "Does anybody see me drowning here?" I thought to myself a million times. I didn't have one person in my life who had admitted to doing drugs or being in a family with someone who did. Still, I was Josiah's mom, his protector, who believed in him and knew who he was. I was his advocate and safe place. Why couldn't I help him get off drugs?

Our family was tight-knit and close. We all cheered for one another no matter the circumstances. There was no reason to think that Josiah wasn't going to bounce back from this mishap. We knew that Josiah had big dreams and a huge appetite for success. We knew nothing could stop him once his mind was set. However, we were ignorant to the world of addiction and chose to believe what we knew of Josiah up until then.

He stayed in his room day after day. I brought him food and drink, making life as comfortable for him as I could. I was totally ignorant and in complete denial. Little by little, things in my home went missing: the Xbox, DVD players, TVs, guns, money, wedding rings, you name it.... Anything of any value disappeared.

Josiah got to the point where he'd only crack his bedroom door enough for me to slide food through to him. He asked me to pay his phone bill and car payment and to put gas in his car, giving me a devastating story about how he was fighting for his life and how sick he was. I believed him and gave him anything he asked. Unwittingly, I was perpetuating the cycle.

One day, he left the house for a bit. I ran up the stairs, wanting to strip the bed and wash the bedding for him. Walking into his room, I just about vomited. Except for a box spring mattress, the room was completely empty. His clothes were gone, as were his nightstand and chest of drawers. There were cups and plates, covered with moldy untouched food. And spoons. I had lost every single spoon in my house, and there they were. I went over and grabbed one. I could see it was burnt.

There were lighters, tiny baggies, and small square pieces of foil all over the room. It reeked of vinegar. There was a shoestring and an orange lid on top of what occurred to me was a needle. Josiah was doing drugs in our house under the guise that he was sick from recovery.

I didn't want to believe it. It was a bad dream I wanted to wake up from. I wanted my Siah back. When I love someone, I have trouble believing the person is a liar. My thought processes weren't being filtered through a logical mind; they were being processed through my emotions and my version of love. I couldn't look at my family members and lie to their faces, so surely Josiah couldn't either. Facing the truth when the truth cuts deep is one of the hardest things we humans have to do. My kids were attached to my identity, so admittance of what was going on meant complete failure and a shattered sense of self.

Meanwhile, Jason buried his head in his work. He and Josiah didn't have a great relationship to start with. When Josiah was using, Jason would get angry and lash out with hurtful, hateful words and, at times, physical violence. Then he would feel guilty, beat himself up for his actions, and go silent. I always thought Jason disengaged at that point. Later, I understood it was just part of the anger cycle. He would try and keep things going by helping Josiah, which was a language I spoke. Then, when Josiah would fall off and start using, Jason would feel overwhelmed, fear setting in, and the cycle would begin again. Jason would express how it felt like he had no self-control over the anger. He felt helpless and therefore ruled by his emotions, so I took on most of the drama solo. The "blow up" that would ensue between the two of them didn't seem worth it, so I stopped telling Jason about every situation regarding Josiah. Jason and I were both simply doing what came naturally—he, working to distract himself from his feelings, and me, handling our kid to distract me from mine.

Jason and I were equally lost as to how to proceed, but we agreed to have a sit-down with Josiah that night. Jason got home and showered, and we decided that Josiah should come downstairs and talk with us. Jason said he would go get Josiah, and off he went up the stairs, counting each step out loud as he went. He didn't knock like I would have, instead, going straight inside unannounced. I could hear Jason's voice elevate through the closed door. His voice got louder and louder, screaming at Josiah to wake up.

I scaled the stairs and pushed the door open, bursting inside. Jason was removing the tourniquet from

Josiah's arm, attempting to shake him awake. The needle fell out of Josiah's arm as a result of Jason's efforts to rouse him. Josiah began to mumble, roused by the shouting. His girlfriend sat up beside him. They didn't share the same room, but we realized then that they shared the same needle.

Jason lost it. He went off on Josiah, telling him how stupid he was and how disappointed we were, demanding this wasn't happening in our house. He told Josiah to get his stuff and get out. By this time, I was crying, searching my mind for words to say to make it all better. There weren't any. Jason's reactions were polar opposite from mine, and in the moment, I believed his reactions were wrong. Jason gathered all the drug paraphernalia and took it out of the house. Josiah and his girlfriend left immediately.

I didn't understand Jason's anger because I was at the opposite end of the spectrum. Addiction has a way of bringing out the core of a person when everything is out of their control. Human nature attempts to take charge of things that seem unmanageable. Fear materialized every time our son used drugs, growing only more monstrous with prolonged use. Jason struggled with fear every day that Josiah used drugs, which for him manifested in yelling and screaming at Josiah, pushing him into walls and speaking words of shame and anger. His exploding anger subsequently destroyed trust and safety.

Jason and I sat outside on the porch swing and considered what we'd do when they returned. We came to the conclusion that I would drive his girlfriend back to Phoenix and separate them in an effort to save them both. However, they didn't come back that night. We had no idea where they'd gone. Forever the optimist, I believed they would return, and I'd take her home and things would get better.

A few days later, we received a call from the police station. They'd both been arrested. Apparently, the police had been keeping an eye on Josiah and knew he was in trouble. They'd already had reason to pull him over, and when they did, they arrested him on a paraphernalia charge and his girlfriend on an outstanding warrant. When Josiah called me, he asked me to get her out of jail and not to worry about him. He must have remembered what I told all my children when they were young: that I would never come bail them out if for any reason they got into trouble.

I hadn't slept in weeks. But, somehow, knowing he was safe and without drugs, I slept like a baby that night. When I woke up in the morning, I picked up his girlfriend and her small bag of clothes and drove her back to the city. I felt a deep desire within me that all this would be put behind us and we'd be back to normal life in no time.

How little I knew. The enormity of the situation had yet to sink into our souls. The fact that we would never know "normal" again didn't even enter our minds.

CHAPTER 3
Shackles

IT WAS MY VERY FIRST TIME IN A COURTROOM, and I had no idea what to expect. Climbing the steep stairs to enter the building and the unknown of what it would bring, I felt anxiety mingled with terror. I walked through the main doors and was met by two officers on the other side of a metal detector. They asked me if I had a phone, though they must have seen it in my hand. No phones were allowed inside. I knew I was early for the proceedings but felt a bit of panic as I hurried down the stairs to my car and back up again.

I didn't have a clue where to go, my eyes searching for signs. I could feel myself getting flushed. The wooden courthouse floors made a scary movie creak with every step I took. I walked up to a man holding a briefcase, thinking he might help direct me. One more flight, he said. I climbed the old staircase, my chest pounding, blood flowing through my body, my steps eerily audible.

I walked in and scanned the courtroom. There were people scattered throughout the room on rickety wooden chairs. I didn't see anyone I recognized. In the front of the room stood a tall wooden desk with a solid front. It looked like every bench I had ever seen in TV courtrooms, complete with the American flag.

In front of the bench were two large tables and two suited men, each rummaging through their respective briefcases. A woman to the left of the bench typed on a computer while a few other women stood against a wall, speaking quietly. There was hushed chatter from various groups of people. I took my seat.

The side door opened, and the sound of rattling chains caught everyone's attention. A jail guard entered first, immediately followed by prisoners in orange jumpsuits, shuffling in tiny steps, feet restricted by chains. The fourth one through the door was Josiah.

My son, my pride and joy, a prisoner in shackles. His dazzling smile caught my eye right away, and I burst into tears. My reaction was so unexpected that I didn't have time to swallow it down, and his facial expression became one of concern, his eyebrows knit together. I was instantly mad at myself and scolded my emotions for leaping out like that. I had learned at a young age that my feelings meant absolutely nothing. Forced to lock them down and bury them deep within my soul, I functioned on sheer obedience, speaking, acting, looking, and thinking as I was told.

At this moment, I felt I needed to be strong for my

son. Bursting into tears showed weakness that I feared would cause him to feel ashamed and desire numbness. I didn't want to be the source of the pain associated with his drug use. He didn't take his eyes off me as I attempted to gain my composure.

I moved my mouth in silence and told him that I loved him, which he mirrored. The guard instructed them to sit as we waited for the judge. By now, the courtroom was dead silent. Josiah kept looking desperately back at me. It caught the attention of the guard, who stood up, approached Josiah, and turned him around.

I realized I hadn't seen his smile in a while. He'd been in jail for a week. That meant he must be sober. The thought surged through me: My Josiah was back. The empty void and blank look had dissipated, replaced by his dancing eyes and huge, dazzling smile.

The judge entered, and we all stood. As prisoners' names were called and charges read, I looked at my son in an orange jumpsuit, shackled. The image continuing to crush me. I kept replaying in my mind the whispered "I love you," the smile…. Hearing "Josiah James Kouts," I was jarred back into reality. He shuffled to the table, glancing back at me with every few tiny steps. The judge read his charges and respective penalties aloud. My stomach was in knots, my swallows were gulps. The judge looked up from his book and began speaking slowly and frankly.

He offered stern words and constructive criticism

before closing his book to stare Josiah dead in his eyes. My heart was pounding. He believed Josiah could beat this addiction. He was willing to give him a chance, sentencing him to six months in rehab. But it was Josiah's responsibility to enroll, and he had six days to do so. The gavel hit the desk, and it was over like that.

Overwhelming emotion hit me. I sobbed, losing all self-control. A flood of relief and hope washed over me. Someone believed in my son and was willing to give him a second chance. Josiah would get the help he needed to beat the addiction.

I followed the jailer and prisoners out of the courtroom. I rushed up to the jailer, asking how I could get Josiah from jail. He didn't say a word. Thankfully, it's a small city, and we know a lot of people. A courthouse employee called my name and told me how everything worked. Her son also struggled with drugs and had been there several times. I saw the motherly pain in her face as she relayed the perils of her son's addiction. He had completed six months in prison, eventually getting out only to relapse and violate his parole. He had a child and girl waiting that whole time. She had lost all hope. She warned me not to set my heart up for my son to be sober because he'd only let me down again and again.

Until that point, no one had talked to me so openly about the painful circumstances I also faced but had yet to fully understand. Her words pierced like razor blades to my heart. It felt like I was beginning to bleed out. So this was life with an addict. She had been dealing with her son's addiction for years and was hurt, downcast, and bitter. She was a beautiful woman, but her countenance was hardened by a heavy fog of pain.

I left her presence with more questions than I'd arrived with. Surely there was something we could do to save our children from this drug. We were just missing the key. It was our duty to find it—they are our children, after all. We must set them free. I filed these fearful thoughts away into the recesses of my mind, burying them to preserve my hope and optimism.

I had a strong desire to save my son, believing he was different from all the other people in the world who injected drugs. I had spent eighteen years with the real Josiah. I knew him inside and out. Being a mom requires loving with pure unadulterated love, and love believes the very best in children. Perhaps a mom's great challenge is overcoming complete denial to see the warning signs and be of even greater service in the name of love.

When he was released, Josiah called me. I immediately went to pick him up. He was a brand new man! He was happy and talked openly about how he'd never touch another drug for as long as he lived. My world was complete again. I felt like we'd dodged the bullet. Jail had woken him up, and I was sure he'd never go down that path again.

Six days after the sentencing, I asked Josiah if he was going to call a center. He assured me that several places would take him once there were available beds. It hadn't occurred to me that he hadn't made a single phone call.

Some weeks went by as if nothing had ever troubled him. We had normal conversations, like old times. He called his girlfriend while she was in Phoenix. They fought constantly, and I realized what a toxic relationship it was. I wanted him to move on and leave the past behind, but he said he loved her. He told me she didn't do drugs, that she'd only ever tried because of him. The following month, he convinced me to pick her up in Phoenix, saying her mom was abusive and didn't want her. That's all it took. I had my own personal experience with issues of abuse, and I wanted the chance to save anyone from it.

CHAPTER 4
The Approaching Storm

I AM IN NO WAY A SELF-PROCLAIMED EXPERT. But I am a mama who educated herself and will help anyone I can.

I applaud those who answer the help hotlines for families struggling with drug use. When I reached out for help, I was informed of what Josiah was facing and just how rampant this issue is. More Americans died last year from a drug overdose than the total number of lives lost in the Vietnam War. There were more than 72,000 overdose deaths in 2017. Between 2011 and 2012, overdose deaths were around 41,500. And this is only the reported cases. Imagine if they were all tested and reported, the numbers would be exponentially higher.

Transparency is so important. Drugs are an epidemic, killing our children and destroying families by the droves. If we had a mass murderer on the loose, shooting people in every city, we'd do whatever it takes to stop him. Drugs are the mass murderer that many people hide and protect, never uttering a word about him. We are a large part of the problem. People fear what they don't understand.

Drug abuse is a misunderstood issue, one we throw stigmas at so we can easily slather shame onto the addicted and their families, subsequently keeping our beliefs safe and the addict hidden. Whatever is hidden doesn't heal, and an addict is as sick as their secrets.

The man I spoke with while finding Josiah help explained how heroin deteriorates the brain's white matter, affecting decision-making abilities, self-regulatory behavior, and stress response. Heroin results in a profound degree of tolerance and physical dependence. Tolerance occurs when increasing amounts of heroin are required to achieve the same effects. Intravenous heroin reaches the brain quickly, providing an almost immediate release into the body. He explained the facial sores and the head-bobbing—"nodding off"—which happens when the user is high. He told me what Josiah's body would go through when it was time to get high again. He educated me on what symptoms came from heroin withdrawal: nausea, vomiting, insomnia, restlessness, muscle and bone pain, cold flashes, and goosebumps. He stated that once addicted to heroin, the addict's entire life revolves around getting the drug.

An intravenous heroin user has a 1% chance of recovery. Once heroin hits the brain, it's converted into morphine and binds rapidly to opioid receptors. The heroin then binds to and activates specific receptors in the brain called mu-opioid receptors (MORs). He explained how our bodies contain naturally-occurring chemicals called neurotransmitters, which bind to these receptors throughout the brain and body to regulate pain, hormone release, and a general sensation of well-being. When MORs are activated in the reward center of the brain, they stimulate the release of the neurotransmitter dopamine, reinforcing the drug-taking behavior. Activating opioid receptors with externally administered opioids such as heroin (versus naturally-occurring chemicals within the body) can cause significant changes to the physical body and brain physiology, leading to long-term neurological and hormonal imbalances that aren't easily reversed.

Opiates are manipulative. They take the user outside of his consciousness. Using them initially feels nostalgic and romantic. The cares of the world seem to vanish as the addict is lured seductively into a death grip. The brain is chemically altered. Heroin pumps in a feeling of euphoria that blocks and numbs pain. The first time is bliss. But soon the bliss isn't enough; the body grows tolerant and requires more and more. Addiction is living with a body fighting for life and a mind toying with death. It's a war from which its soldiers return radically altered, if at all. No one wants to go through the hell of withdrawal, so the addict chases the high like his life depends on it.

Addiction is all-consuming. It turns life's aim into

getting money for drugs, using the drugs, and not getting caught in the process. Using becomes the main reason for living. All the drugs get used up, and the cycle starts all over again. More have to be acquired at all costs. Waiting longer than necessary isn't an option, so a nearby bathroom is used for shooting up; dealers are called the moment money comes in at midnight; drawers are ransacked and floors crawled in the hope of finding a dropped pill or loose change. Addiction is an impatient leech that demands feeding.

With Josiah, that meant I didn't hear his laugh anymore. I didn't hear him speak of his future or all the things he would accomplish. His thriving spirit was gone, replaced by the desire to be numb and do whatever it took to get there. Looking back, I get it. I know what it's like to want to numb the pain. It's hard to put into words how I feel as I remember the pain of bringing him into the world subsided the moment the drugs administered entered my body, and here my baby is now desiring nothing more than to numb his own pain.

I was even more determined to speak life into my son somehow. I would try to appeal to his rational mind, but drugs had it underwater. He couldn't hear my words, no matter how many ways I phrased them. Damaged by constant drug abuse, he lacked any sense of awareness, feeling, or motivation. The Josiah who remained was emotionally, psychologically, and spiritually crippled. Once called "preacher kid," he now questioned his faith. When we are hurting, we hurt others. God is the easiest to turn on in those times.

Drugs took Josiah's faith. He would say, "If there is a God, why isn't He intervening? He left me high and dry. I can't imagine a loving God allowing me to go through this. I've seen way too much evil to believe there's a God who loves someone like me. Mom, you can't expect me to believe in those ancient Bible writings. You believe in God because that's what someone told you to believe." Josiah's faith—mine as well, I'd soon realize—was in a god constructed by our fallible, skewed thinking. It was a faith shaped by cracked goggles, a view of things not as they are but as we are.

Although I was quickly learning that enabling Josiah was hurting him, I knew I would never turn my back on him. No matter how he acted, I had to keep believing, trusting he'd get well and would be back to the old Josiah, to before the drugs. As a mom, that's what love does. I'd believe in him all over, again and again.

My loving stance and willingness to believe were continually challenged not only by Josiah himself but also by my family, friends, and community.

When going through addiction and everything it entails, everyone seemed to have an answer for me. Though that isn't to say that a single person actually opened up to me about any personal experience of theirs. As the parent of an addict, it's the same advice from every person I talk to. The answers are fear-filled and hopeless. Not one person I encountered gave me a glimpse of hope. Most days I was the only one who believed in and remembered who my son was before drugs. All the while, everyone else was seeing my son through the lens of his addiction.

We live in a small community, where religion is prevalent and most people only offer their highlight reels. Shame is cast on families dealing with addiction issues, and the community withdraws. The addict may be battling with Satan himself, but then, add to that the fight with a community that views him as garbage to be taken out and discarded. The family of the addict is pressured to save face by getting rid of the problem.

Thing is, addicts come from all walks of life and all types of families. Drugs don't discriminate. They don't discern age, race, social status, or gender. They're happy to claim you in whatever state.

I realized I had once been one of those people. I had so feared what I didn't understand that I judged instead of educating myself. The judgment wasn't such an easy one when it landed in my family, myself now the recipient of the persecution I once doled out as easily as taking a breath.

On many occasions, it was too painful to think Josiah might be using again. It was easier to deny it and tell myself I was being suspicious. So I made excuses for his behavior and pretended he was fine, blinded by the shame and guilt I felt for being a parent whose child had become addicted to drugs.

No parent aspires to raise a drug addict. In attempting to deal with something I didn't understand,

I tried to wrap my brain around what was happening. My child, my flesh and blood, was taking a drug that was killing him before my very eyes.

It's as if the drug is in the corner doing push-ups, waiting for the addict to feel weak. When that weak moment comes, the drug is there knocking, offering anesthetic against the pressures and hardships of life. The drug presents itself as a best friend, the one who can make the cruel world disappear, taking precedence over everything.

It seemed whenever I believed Josiah was finished with the drug that was ruining his whole life, he'd go right back to it. Using became his answer to hardships. It rendered coping skills nonessential. I know Josiah loved his family and hated hurting us, but he didn't want to feel the pain of life. Addiction overrides everything the addict knows is right and takes over every aspect of life. You can't just stop shooting heroin and return everything back to normal. The chemistry of the brain is forever altered.

Drugs inhibit maturation and are emotionally crippling. Talking to an addict is like talking to a walking contradiction. Words are twisted in so many ways that it's near impossible to keep a sane head during conversation. Addicts' actions are erratic and nonsensical. When you question their behavior, even out of love and concern, that concern is spun around on you until you're the bad guy and, as their protector, added to their list of demons to fight.

Addicts are master manipulators. They can twist scenarios in many ways. They pick fights, and then they use your reaction as fuel to give them another excuse to use. Over and over again, the naive observer plays the same hand with an addict. We react with judgment and shame, we remain ignorant and in denial, and we're incapable of supporting those we love most. This shame cycle perpetuates the addiction, begetting further dysfunction and driving the addict further away.

Many perfectly good people will tell you to turn your back on an addict, to tell the addict what a piece of crap he is and give him no more access to your life. I've talked to many parents who have this problem of either enabling or using "shaming" words. It's a constant, never-ending cycle of dysfunction, and it brings forth no life.

Life with an addict is like being on a merry-go-round. You go around and around and get nowhere. Daily life is filled with drama and turmoil. A person on drugs, once such a kind and honest person, behaves reprehensibly and erratically, exhibiting actions that are calloused and mean. The addict will do whatever it takes to prevent withdrawal. Similarly, enablers will do whatever it takes to prevent feeling scared or out of control, often leading to further enabling. Sober parents may be their children's caregivers, their only hope, their beacon home in the fiercest of storms… but this isn't a merry-go-round they are naturally equipped to ride.

Much like addicts don't grow emotionally, psycho-logically, or spiritually, their loved ones tend to be lured into similar behavior. Our family didn't intentionally stop growing, but the addiction that infiltrated us took over our entire existence. We were thrown into a whirlwind of drama, an emotional rollercoaster that left us vulnerable and on high alert.

"Give all your worries and cares
to God, for He cares about
what happens to you."
— 1 Peter 5:7

DAILY LIFE CAME with a new set of terrors. It involved trying to separate truth from lies, sometimes deciphering a mixture of both. When the truth would have been easier to tell, Josiah would lie. One day, he was positive he hadn't touched anyone's belongings; the next day, he'd admit to having "borrowed" them and had no idea where they would have gone.

While actively addicted, my son took us on the ride of our lives. We had to lock up all of the household medications. Every day, the house was hit by a hurricane of Josiah rummaging for anything that could be sold. I was caught in a disturbing cycle of thoughts: Is my son dead or sleeping? Can I invite friends over? Will he steal something or embarrass us with his erratic behavior? Why is my son running on the roof at three in the morning? Why are the police calling me? Why is there blood on the floor?

There were the constant stories painting him as the victim whom no one would help. Mood swings came in epic proportion with no consistency from one moment to the next. One day, Josiah would be happy as a lark; the next, he'd spend crying, depressed, or angry. He had days when he didn't trust anyone around him, certain everyone was out to get him. He would be mean to his girlfriend and accuse her of horrible things. We never knew what would trigger him and the extent of his thinking until his actions became apparent.

They say that drug addiction becomes a family disease. Addiction is a relationship, pathologically binding to the addict and replacing the actual people who matter. The family sees the drug killing the addict and wants to help in any way possible, jumping in, in an attempt to kill off the perpetrator. The addict views interference as sabotage to his object of obsession, driving him deeper into the clutches of the drug-relationship.

When addiction hit our family, a plethora of emotions subsequently followed. It felt like we were drowning in the fiercest of seas, using all our time and energy to stay above water. The waves never stop hitting. There's no reprieve from the feeling of drowning. At this point, as a means of survival, many families wipe their hands clean of their addicts, or else they numb themselves, instead, by drowning in work, liquor, or gambling or in feelings of bitterness, hatred, and malice. I understand. My mind told me it's more than any human can take, and my heart desperately needed a break from the feelings impaling it.

As messed up as I was, emotions hijacked and spirit crushed, I didn't want to hide our difficulties from others. I no longer wanted to feel ashamed to say I had a drug addict son or that our family was proud of Josiah and would continue to believe in him. My daughter and son would defend him tirelessly. Doing so became an aspect of our family's daily pressure.

Addicts, on the other hand, want the addiction to be kept secret, not wanting to be seen at all. They isolate themselves in the hopes that their lives are hidden and secluded.

Our family was at a crossroads: choose to escape or choose to fight; make others uncomfortable with talk of drug addiction or keep silent and watch it kill. As contradictory as it may sound, fighting would require us to educate ourselves in the midst of the raging sea of our lives. Fighting would mean letting our son go and giving him to God. We had to dig deep, dig outside of our emotions and feelings. We had to focus and think logically, despite every circumstance around us attempting to take us under.

Little did we know, the approaching storm would hit our family with hurricane force.

CHAPTER 5

Chasing the Dragon

JASON AND I DESIRED JOSIAH'S SOBRIETY more than he did. Maintaining a high prevents the addict from getting "dope sick," which entails severe pain, skin-crawling sensations, sweats, diarrhea, stomach cramps, anxiety, and more. Each time Josiah detoxed, he felt like he was locked in a tiny box unable to move or breathe. He went through countless detoxes with me at home, after the drugs had made him so miserable he was sure he wanted off. Each time, it was torture to watch. This went on for the entire journey of his addiction. I attribute the detox periods to prayer. We would pray so hard that he'd be miserable and without peace in his addiction.

As such novices to the drug world, detox seemed like the answer we needed. Detox doesn't mean the addiction stops. Physical addiction is nowhere near as dangerous as mental addiction. Nearly everyone can relate to and likely suffers from mental addiction.

Mental addiction is how we convince ourselves to "get a hit" even though we don't want to, even though it will hurt us and everyone around us. This can come in the form of addiction to control, codependency, shopping, work, checking our devices every few minutes. Mental addictions—like physical addiction—do not discriminate and come in all shapes and sizes. Often, they can go undetected because there are no obvious physical symptoms.

By this point, Josiah never went long periods of time on drugs. He would relapse, but soon he'd want off again to be free from the "dragon." During one relapse, I insisted he go to a detox center, personally calling and getting him into one about an hour and a half away from home. I set up the time, and off we went. When we arrived, the lady at the desk was busy and Josiah was super antsy, fidgety, and restless. He said he needed a cigarette, and he and I stepped outside. Minutes later, the lady came outside and told us smoking was prohibited on the premises. She told Josiah she was ready to see him, and with a tearful hug and Josiah's assurance that he'd be fine, I jumped in my car and headed home.

Josiah didn't want food before going into detox, so I was famished after dropping him off. I stopped at a fast-food chain and sat inside, finally able to take a deep breath and calm my broken heart. I had once again looked into my son's desperate, pain-filled eyes and handed him a solution. I believed that if he were sober, he could live pain-free, and I would do whatever it took to get him there. I didn't want to admit that the reason he wasn't sober was because he was trying to numb the pain he felt as so many of us do. It was hard to know if taking him to get help was enabling or loving him. Was he at rock bottom, wanting help, as he claimed? Or was he playing me because he knew I wanted sobriety more than he did?

My son was so close to me that I couldn't make an unbiased, educated decision about detox or anything else. I couldn't force myself to pull back and let him figure it out on his own. Once he said he was done, I was all in.

I arrived home in the late afternoon, and there sat Josiah on the porch swing. How did he beat me home? I jumped out of my car, angry and confused. He told me the lady was rude and that he wasn't allowed to use his phone or keep any of his belongings. He said she used abusive language and there was no way he could get help there. "Now what?" I thought to myself, "What solution can I come up with to help him get clean?"

In the next few days, I got a call from one of the men who worked at the detox facility, himself a recovering addict. I told him Josiah's experience at the detox center, and he asked me to bring him back. He said he would speak to Josiah and see to it that he got the best help. He wanted to share his story with Josiah and aid in his sobriety all he could. I was thrilled, much more so than Josiah.

This same scenario happened over and over. He'd get sober and grow resolute never to touch a drug again. I'd gladly take him to detox after detox, each time believing this time would be the last. We went all over the state of Arizona. Then Josiah started finding the places, going to medical facilities that would give him either Suboxone or Methadone without my knowledge. I would drop him off, wait for his call, and go pick him up four or five days later.

I have never believed that a drug can cure you from a drug. A shopping addict won't be cured at the dollar store, simply spending less. The treatment would be to find out what is broken inside that causes the compulsion. Suboxone and Methadone are simply smaller dosages of the drug. They didn't cure what was going on inside Josiah.

In later years, Josiah told me it was a million times worse to get off Suboxone and Methadone than it was to get off of heroin. We chased detox centers as bad as Josiah chased the heroin dealer, if not worse. As an enabler, you'll chase anything that looks like help. On Suboxone, Josiah's behavior grew worse than it ever had been on heroin.

Jason and a few friends had gone on a two-night hike a couple hours from where we live. I was home and Josiah was upstairs in his room. I could hear thuds and slams amid Josiah's elevated voice. I went up to his room and heard him yelling through his cracked door. He was naked. I asked him what was going on, and he began pounding his head against the wall over and over. I grabbed him to hold him back, but he over-powered me. He was yelling that he hated his life and wanted to be dead. He fell to the floor and placed his hands on the carpet, slamming his head on the floor. I asked him what drug he was taking. In true drug ad-dict fashion, he said he wasn't taking any. He was so out of it that he didn't protest as I searched his things: his socks, the mattress, the box-spring, the ceiling fan, the insides of books and lotion containers, his tooth-paste, backpacks, deodorant sticks.... Addicts have the best hiding places you can imagine.

I found some white strips I had never seen before. I looked on both sides for a name or any details that might identify what they were. Before I knew it, Josiah snatched them out of my hand. He peeled off the back of an entire paper containing what looked to be ten strips and ate them all.

Over and over again, he hit his head against what-ever hard surface he was near, ran through his bath-room and then back through the hallway into his bed-room. I went to grab him some shorts to put on and he jumped in the shower, slamming his head into the marble walls. My first instinct was to turn on the water to try and get him to stop. He jumped out of the show-er, dripping wet, and ran out of his room. I chased him downstairs and stopped him from going out the front door. All the while he was screaming that he wanted to die. I forced him onto the couch and wrapped a blanket around him, attempting to speak logic to him and begging him to trust what I was saying. I pulled every ounce of strength I had in me and poured it into him.

He argued at first, high and dazed from repeatedly hitting his head. It gave me the upper hand. The effects of the Suboxone fully hit him, and he was in and out of hysteria and consciousness. We sat on the couch for some hours, my legs wrapped around his tiny frame and my arms holding him with all my might.

Eventually, he calmed completely. He stopped struggling and asked if he could smoke a cigarette. Although his words were almost unintelligible, I told him that if he sat still, I'd run upstairs and grab him a cigarette. When I got back to him, he attempted to stand and make his way to the front door. What with the Suboxone overdose and the abuse his head had sustained, he could barely walk.

I wrapped his arm around my neck and walked him out the front door to sit him down on the porch swing. I lit his cigarette and told him I had to run to the bathroom. I grabbed my cell phone and began desperately dialing everyone I could think of who could come help me. Not a single person I called answered. It was one in the morning by then. I was operating on instinct rather than rationality, and it didn't occur to me that I should have called 911. I stayed up all night with him, making sure he was still breathing. After twelve or so hours, he began coming out of the effects, but that meant his body would only crave more. The cycle would start again. I was alone and terrified.

The next day, my cell phone rang. It was Jason. He had just reached a cell service area. Hearing his voice, I went into hysterics. My call scared him so much that he drove 90 miles per hour on a dirt road to get home. His friends later told me they feared for their lives in that car.

Josiah was calm when Jason got home. I was anything but. Suffering from sheer emotional and physical fatigue, navigating a situation I didn't understand at all, I was without a rational mind. I was mad and scared and felt like everything was out of my control. Instead of seeing the situation for what it truly was, I was preoccupied with hurt for having to go through it alone. I felt like Jason had abandoned me, Instead of seeing the problem as Josiah's, I made it into mine and Jason's.

Part of being an enabler is feeling like I have to handle difficulties because my loved one isn't capable of doing so. As everything went to hell, my identity was so fragile that I couldn't carry the weight of it all. I withdrew from Jason, going into shutdown mode to protect myself from the horrors I had experienced. Trauma and misplaced identity took me to an unhealthy place in an attempt to protect that which was most fragile. Burying my pain deep down inside of me made it feel bearable at the moment. I have come to understand that our lives are often like an iceberg; we are aware of only a fraction of them and largely unaware of the hidden mass beneath the surface. The hidden mass wreaks havoc on our lives. Hidden things never heal, and in order to expose our "hidden" feelings and emotions, we have to admit that they are beyond our control and in desperate need of the Father's touch. If we don't bring our feelings and emotions to the surface, we remain in repeated cycles of pain and addiction, resulting in emotional numbness.

This is how addiction becomes a family disease.

Josiah awoke with the initial reaction of grief for what he had put me through. His remorse quickly turned into shame. Remorse would have made him feel the weight of his actions. An emotional cripple, he quickly dodged that and set out to find drugs. Jason yelled and screamed about how stupid his decisions were. In Jason's mind, he was trying to save his life. Josiah didn't view it that way.

Jason has what some call a direct, "get 'er done my way or the highway" personality. He's quick to react, which is a strength in many ways, but he found the trait sabotaged his endeavors to deal with our son. From a young age, Josiah desperately wanted to please Jason. But Josiah took after his mom in personality, the polar opposite of his dad. Jason, a hard-working man his whole life, attempted to instill those traits in Josiah. He had dreamt of his firstborn following in his footsteps to one day take over the family construction business. Josiah, on the other hand, learned early on that he preferred to use his brain and not his brawn, displaying no interest in construction whatsoever. It wrecked Jason's expectations of Josiah.

Jason's love language wasn't one Josiah understood. Josiah was a lover, never a fighter. He was a deep feeler and would make peace at all costs, an empath at his very core who felt pain when he hurt others. He was emotional in a very soft way. Conversely, Jason was also very emotional, in a quick, heated, passionate, fiery way. Jason's emotions always seemed out of control. Jason loves deeply, but his way of projecting love was so different from Josiah's. He'd raise his voice and yell out of passionate engagement, even if it came across as intimidating. His way of expressing love shut Josiah down.

Jason eventually learned that his ways of "handling" Josiah's addiction were pushing his son away instead of drawing him closer. His road to healing, like mine, came along with falling many times. But our minds weren't hijacked by heroin, so we would get back up with more resolve than before and keep trying. Jason would hold his tongue and extend his arms.

Where there is anger, there is always pain underneath. Our anger tells us where we feel powerless. It doesn't solve anything, but it has the power to destroy everything. Mean words can scar a person for life. The emotions that come from anger represent the most present, pressing, painful force in our lives. When trust has been wrecked by anger, it's a slow process of healing, but if we stay true to the course, healing does come. Jason learned to speak a little softer, putting down his stick. Josiah could tell his dad was trying. Even on drugs, he never stopped being perceptive, and Jason's efforts never failed to soften him.

When Josiah had time away from his dad, he could process the many ways Jason was displaying the love that he hadn't seen before. Over time, he recognized that Jason had many regrets that held him captive with guilt. Josiah loved so much, and he went through a great deal to make his dad feel appreciated and loved.

Days later, Josiah again played the card that never failed. He showed up at home and said he was finished with drugs and needed a ride to a detox center. I dropped everything going on in my life to save his. I got the call five days later, again dropping everything to pick him up from detox. He was always so happy to see me, his famous smile melting me to my core. He spoke all the words a mama wants to hear, and I believed every one of them.

He probably told me a thousand times that he'd never touch drugs again. And every time he relapsed and went to detox, he told me his brain didn't function like it used to. He continually said he'd never be able to return to who he once had been. I didn't believe it for a second. In my mind, he was resilient and would beat this, period.

Each time I took him to detox, I believed he needed to go because he felt a craving for the dragon. He would later tell me he never actually stopped using heroin and only wanted the Suboxone for the moments he didn't have the funds for heroin, that it helped with his withdrawal symptoms until he could procure more. Once I understood the concept of enabling, I came to view my dysfunction as grave as his, as if I was sticking the needle in my arm right alongside him. Initially, it was much too painful to process, as much as I tried to mask my fragility with strength. It took me over a year to really process it all.

I took him to a facility in the Phoenix area. We were sitting together waiting for someone to check him in when a young man came in and got the clerk's attention right away. She addressed him by name, asking, "You're back when we just released you last night?" "Last night?!" I thought. "What on earth would he be doing back so quickly? I'm so glad Josiah doesn't do that." How naive I was to the dragon I was facing, yet to realize the lure of something that could promise him what I never could: numbness.

Those initial months seemed like years. It was a crash course on the effects of addiction on a family. Our family unit stopped functioning in its normal capacity. We stopped celebrating birthdays, special occasions, and other reminders of life as Josiah and his needs took precedence over everything. For six long months, it was detox center after detox center, trying to resurrect my son.

CHAPTER 6

Fighting Together

ALL ENABLERS LOVE SOMEONE who is out of control. To the extent that the enabled is unwilling to take responsibility for his own actions, the enabler overcompensates by getting inappropriately involved. I was disturbed and deeply affected by what my son was doing. I didn't know how to cope with my child being totally out of my control. He wasn't the only sick one: I had created the environment in which my son was held hostage. Six months in, I realized I had to get help.

It was a lonely six months. I didn't know anyone who had walked the road I was on. I attended a small church and the parishioners were as scared as I was, unable to offer hope or instruction. Lacking a framework for how to proceed, I felt hopeless and lost.

Some friends advised me to show him tough love, but I didn't know what tough love was. My mind would sink into the ditch of my childhood and quickly turn back. I browsed the internet day and night for answers. I was desperate to save my son's life, not yet desperate to save my own. I still felt I had to be involved in Josiah's process of getting clean. I didn't think it could happen without me. I was sick, mentally and psychologically. I needed to be lord of our lives. As a mom, I was only as good as my kids were.

All of my time and energy went into helping Josiah. There was no limit to my willingness to fight off the perpetrator. Fun outings had ceased. Dinner plans were canceled in anticipation of Josiah's inevitable tantrums and interruptions. Our only celebrations were for Josiah coming home sober. Our conversations, our lives, centered around Josiah and how to help him.

Sitting at Pizza Hut one time, my daughter stunned me when she suddenly asked, "Mom, you do know you have two other kids, right?" I didn't realize what I had done, that I'd shoved them to the side and made them ghosts in our home. I know their voices were muffled and needs overlooked amid all the drama of addiction. I committed to trying harder. But they were so strong, they didn't need me like Josiah did…. I would slip right back into making Josiah the center of my world. He took all my time, money, energy, and attention.

Montana and Austin loved Josiah and would do anything in the world for him. Josiah was the funny, popular, happy older brother who made their little world adventurous in their youth. He was the ringleader of all their new ideas and make-believe games. They'd

66

pretend to shoot each other, turning off all the lights in the house and sneaking around hiding. Bursts of shouts and laughter filled the home on a constant basis: "You didn't get me! You missed!" "No, I got you, you're it!"

Josiah loved to tease and get the other two riled up. They were normal siblings with normal arguments and a lot of love. When all three of them got together, arguments always ensued. They were usually started by Josiah, who loved to instigate, watching their reactions and laughing like it was his greatest accomplishment of the day. When we moved into our two-story house, Josiah would stand upstairs and throw his underwear on Montana or Austin's head as they sat on the couch downstairs. Their reactions made him belly laugh with joy before running away in feigned shock when I'd tell him to stop.

Once Josiah got on drugs, he was a different brother. He started stealing from his siblings. Anything that held value that he knew he could sell, he stole. Since we had never been around drugs and didn't know anything about them, none of us knew to lock up our things.

Ever since addiction hit our family, I was totally derailed, my vision focused almost exclusively on my son drowning. I dove in after him, and he took me (and everyone else) under. What I needed was someone to throw me a life preserver, not jump in after me.

I've heard horror stories of sober children resenting

their parents so much for being consumed with the addict child that they walk away. I am among what I believe are the few who have amazing kids who remained unconditionally loving and kind despite being ghosts in our home. Montana and Austin never expressed resentment toward me for being consumed by Josiah's addiction. They didn't question my judgment or act out to get my attention. They rolled with each new set of terrors and stood by me, never guilting or shaming me for helping Josiah so much. They never once acted embarrassed by their brother, though I never explicitly asked if they were. They fought hard against people smearing their brother's name. They went through the process like the amazing champs they are.

I didn't understand until much later that we were all thrown in the deep end together, all of us going in circles because we were naive to what was happening. Their lives paused while our family fought the addiction. When Josiah finally went to rehab, the other two had to go with us to see him on the weekends. Their time became Josiah time, just like mine did.

Though they'd have plenty of bumps and hardships ahead, my children would navigate them. I see that Montana and Austin both struggle with trust. When trust is broken by a sibling, it's easy to be skeptical of anyone who says they love you. My kids were leading me even though they might have felt invisible. They had taken a back seat for a year and ended up being a beacon for their mom. They told me and Jason what great parents we were through it all. They didn't put the dissatisfaction of the past year on our shoulders, leaving those events out as though our family had never skipped a step.

For any siblings of addicts: jump off the merry-go-round and don't let it suck you back on. You have the potential to be the light, a signal for your parents to jump off. My kids are living proof of that. Understand that your parents are doing the only thing they know how to do under the circumstances. Don't be mad at them for fighting. Your parents view you as strong and capable, and, in the end, you're a much better person when your parents view you this way. You'll make it through this period in your family's life. You can be successful and have a wonderful life. You aren't dependent on another person. You are responsible and take care of your daily existence. You are strong and courageous and have full control of your life.

It's amazing how we can grow when that's what's expected of us. As guilt-stricken as I was for checking out on my kids, I saw how both of them were taking on life. Montana lived at home for the first six months of Josiah's addiction before deciding to take a job abroad for a year. I'll always be thankful for the time she spent in Australia, which matured her and made her responsible as well as got her off the merry-go-round and allowing her to grow in every area of life.

Austin quit high school a year early and got his GED.

He started working for his dad full-time and kept busy with friends and hobbies after work. It was a great outlet for him and, like Montana, he grew leaps and bounds that year. He bought a brand new truck, took on payments and insurance, and got a cell phone. He was thrown into the deep end, and he swam.

Together as a family, we had to jump off the merry-go-round and stay off at all costs. We had to fight to keep our family intact. Fighting would mean choosing to be part of the solution, not part of the disease. In the drug world, fighting means surrendering everything we think we know and unlearning everything that feels natural.

That isn't an easy thing to do, especially when it comes to times full of family and traditions.

> "The Lord hears His people
> when they call to Him for help.
> He rescues them from all their
> troubles."
>
> — Psalm 34:17

IT WAS THE HOLIDAY SEASON, and the smell of wood burning in fireplaces filled the air. The leaves had begun to change, and the day's light cut shorter. Our house was filled with decorations. Bright orange pumpkins, maroon flowers, a wreath on the wall, beautiful fall tables, and candles set a warm, cozy mood. Nights and early mornings were crisp while Jason and I enjoyed our cups of coffee, wrapped in nice, fluffy blankets. Autumn had always been one of my favorite seasons.

Josiah had convinced me to let him and his girlfriend move into a travel trailer parked just outside our house. He assured me they were free of drugs and wanted to be mature and live on their own. He had a job cleaning carpets and would assume responsibility for his own welfare.

We'd gone through months of hell, but the tides seemed to be turning. Jason and I were busy at work during the day and lived at basketball games in the evening. I was working at a gym, coaching and teaching Zumba. Jason was building homes and taking care of his construction business. Our family appeared to be bouncing back from the arduous trials we had endured. Austin would bring a handful of kids home on the evenings he didn't have games, and they'd ride their bikes in our backyard. Jason built them ramps and turned the yard into a skate park. Austin was a stud basketball player, and his season had just begun.

Montana was more of a one-friend-at-a-time kind of girl, and she had her bestie over constantly. It was Montana's senior year, and she had a pretty light schedule during the day but a full basketball schedule at night. I chased my kids all over the state of Arizona to watch them play ball.

Jason was a basketball official and was sent to various locations, making it nearly impossible for me to watch him officiate. During basketball season, we were seldom home. Eating in had become a thing of the past. I had no time to prepare meals, nor did we have time to be home for a sit-down dinner.

We knew from the absence of his car that Josiah was getting up and going to work in the mornings. When we were home, we'd find his laundry in the washer or dryer. He was functioning like a normal adult, or so we thought.

Jason had the night off, and we went out to a local restaurant for dinner with some friends we hadn't seen in a year or two. Suddenly, Jason's phone rang. He answered, and his face quickly turned from smiling to concerned. He jumped up from the table and told me to stay put. He assured me he'd be back, offering no explanation of what happened or where he was going.

I sat in the restaurant with our friends, and the pit in my belly instantly took away my appetite. It would be an hour before Jason came back to get me. He apologized to the friends and said that it was an emergency and he didn't want to spoil the evening. We said our goodbyes and headed for the car. I was filled with panic as I asked Jason what had happened.

It was Austin who had called. Josiah's girlfriend told him that Josiah and his cousins were "messed up bad." They had told her to get out, and she ran in and told Austin. Austin barged into the trailer to see all three of them shooting up.

Jason arrived home and threw open the trailer door. He shoved Josiah against the wall and started screaming at him. He began ransacking the whole trailer. There were needles, baggies, and foils everywhere. The entire time he was yelling and screaming, all three boys denied doing drugs.

Austin was fourteen years old and being exposed to the putrid smell of vinegar and the sight of his brother and cousins high with needles in their arms. I was the one who told Josiah he could live in the trailer. I was the one responsible for aiding my son, first, in killing himself with drugs and, now, in exposing the horrors of his actions to my youngest.

Later that night, Jason told me what happened. "I'm done," I declared. Jason asked me what I meant. For the very first time, I was completely resolute in my decision. I was done enabling my son. I knew in that moment that it was the right thing to do. I didn't know, though, how truly hard it would be to stay free of what I had spent years mistaking as love.

I had to love my oldest in an extremely unnatural way. I couldn't believe his words, but I had to believe wholeheartedly in him. I had to remove my grasp and let him fall. I stopped paying his debts in town; he would have to figure out how to get to work and the gym all by himself. He'd have to clean his room, make his own food, buy his own cigarettes, pay for gas and his phone. Jason also had to do what was unnatural, speaking words of belief and continuing to speak them even when Josiah messed up. Fighting meant surrendering what felt natural and instead doing what would be best for everyone.

CHAPTER 7
We Call It Love

PEOPLE WOULD OFTEN SPEAK TO ME about "tough love." I was sadly misled by what that turned out to mean, hearing them say I should give up on him, boot him to the curb, kick him out of my life. I couldn't do that. No matter what. In the first months of having my addict son in my home, I completely enabled him.

It wasn't the first time. I'm an enabler by nature. I enabled him throughout his childhood, stepping in to save him in countless circumstances, learning too late when my son should do something for himself. When he would want to help me in the kitchen, I'd take over. I would run beside him so he never fell when learning to ride a bike. I was a helicopter mom that monitored his every move so he wouldn't experience anything bad happening. I overcompensated for his lacking or dysfunctional relationship with his dad. But this episode—having my youngest find him with a needle stuck in his arm—knocked abrupt sense into me.

I've always felt that I have a way of seeing people. I can meet someone for the first time and feel their pain at the initial touching of hands. Some may say it's a gift, but it often feels like a curse. I feel deeply for people and want to save the world from hardships and unpleasant consequences. If I could, I would rescue every last hurting soul. If I had it my way, the world would be without crises. Three little lives, in particular, I could focus on saving.

My first loves, my "mini-mes," my babies—completely dependent on their mama—gave me purpose each day. I would spend years protecting what was most valuable to me. My children are my entire life, my reason for existence. I pride myself on being a good mom and an even better protector, picking my children up when they fall, cleaning their cuts, nursing them on sick days. I'd stay up all hours of the night, rocking them and giving them fever medicine. I taught them how to walk and talk, count and color. I taught them shapes and how to brush their teeth. Regarding everything essential in their little lives, I was a willing participant in their development. Being a mom gave me an identity I had never had before. I had influence over and a voice in my babies' lives, and they trusted and listened to me.

My instinct as a mom is to save my children from hardships, to protect them at all costs from being "left alone" to be hurt and damaged by the real consequences of their actions. My heart is ripped to pieces at the thought of children being teased or bullied, especially if an adult doesn't step in to help. Of course, I disciplined my kids, but I refused to let anyone else, especially the world at large, do so. I viewed others' discipline as abuse.

I love helping, assisting, supporting, and bailing my kids out of trouble. My kids are extensions of me; I take responsibility for their actions and feel anxious and uneasy when they face any negative consequences. Enabling, I realized, is essentially love turned into fear. I provide help, but what I'm actually doing is exercising control, playing God in the lives of those I love most. I didn't realize it at the time, but I made my children codependent on me.

Having deemed myself my kids' problem solver, I took it upon myself to find solutions to their issues. I didn't want any unnecessary weight on their shoulders. I didn't want them to spend their lives recovering from me and my decision not to protect them, as I had spent a lifetime recovering from my upbringing. My own childhood trauma and feelings of neglect and abandonment led me to raise my children in the completely opposite manner. Instead of finding a middle ground— true functionality—I swung to the other extreme.

I had good kids, and I would see to it that life and everyone in life treated them well. I made their lives as happy and fulfilled as I possibly could. Life was an endless party, a big happy place where everyone got along and played nice. I wouldn't allow them to experience the cold, harsh world of hate and prejudice. As it turns out, no one is immune, even under the best circumstances and with the best intentions. We can only do our best and trust God to handle the rest.

Enabling looks and sounds like love, but its consequences are life-shattering. The enabled child becomes an adult who doesn't know how to take responsibility for his actions or fulfill the normal roles of adulthood. I figured life out for my kids, paving the way for happiness and enjoyment. Their entire lives, I put the proverbial needle in my arm and called it love. In hindsight, it was grossly dysfunctional. I crippled my children.

Here are some common things an enabler will say:

"If I can keep my loved one from going through what I went through, I will do so at all costs."

"They had a reason for doing what they did; as a parent, it's my job to protect them from the pain of that action."

"I know he raced down the highway, but he's a boy. I can't let them mark up his record for a mistake. I'll get him an attorney and fix this mess."

"Every time my child fights with his or her spouse, my child leaves and comes home. I know it could escalate, so I provide a way of escape. I wish my child would leave for good."

"If I kick him out, he'll be homeless. He could die! The world won't love or protect him—that's my job."

The opposite of enabling is anger. In our family, I

was the enabler and my husband was the anger. There are so many roots of anger: panic, worry, frustration, confusion, overwhelmedness, shock, vulnerability, rejection.... All of them manifest in the same reaction. Dealing with an addict child, I believe fear is the number one emotion that manifests in anger. The harsh reality of a loved one's possible death from drugs hits hard and ferociously. Protection turns to fear and worry and exhibits itself in anger.

When addiction struck our family, we immediately went into "saving the addict" mode, highlighting who we are at the level of our deepest fears and insecurities. We quickly realized that the addict is completely out of our scope of understanding, and we lost our minds trying to understand his. When understanding his mind hit a dead end, fear, panic, and pain sank into our souls, and those emotions reemerge as anger.

For the first six months of Josiah's addiction, Jason was angry and vocal, whereas I was enabling and vocal. Both of our positions on the emotional spectrum came from deep-seated fear. I'd attempt to make Jason see things my way, and he'd do the same. We both loved our son with all our hearts and did what came naturally, in the end only adding to the dysfunction of addiction.

All this time, I feared hurting my son by being hands-off, struck by overwhelming anxiety and panic at the thought. It took hitting rock bottom to realize I wasn't helping him. What's more, I wasn't loving him.

Enabling is not loving. In turn, stopping enabling is not stopping loving. I had wanted so badly to help my son. Learning what healthy help looks like, I realized I had yet to do so.

We live in a small community where everyone knows everyone. Jason had been involved in local politics for years and was known by the majority of local business owners. When Josiah would steal from a local business, Jason and I would get a call. At first, I cleaned up his messes. But, one step at a time, I stopped intervening and allowed Josiah to take responsibility. I had to remind myself constantly: his choices are his own, and so are his consequences.

Josiah spent his paychecks on frivolous things, expecting me to pay for his gas and food. I stopped providing him that. He had to figure it out himself. When he told me he didn't have a ride to work, I'd reply, "You'd better run, or you're going to be late" When he asked to borrow my car to go to the gym, I'd say no. Eventually, I stopped taking him to detox after detox after detox. He'd tell me I was petty and selfish, but I stuck to my guns.

My education process taught me that a parent can and should speak life and destiny to the addict. Words of encouragement and motivation say we'll never give up believing in them and serve as their beacon home. We're the ones who remember who our children really are, while others see them through the lens of addiction and related behavior. We can provide encouragement and coaching, keeping in mind that our brains aren't hijacked by drugs. We can also provide contact information on rehabilitation centers and drug counselors but don't force this help. It's unhealthy to force people to do something so we feel better. It has to be their decision.

Lavish your addict with love words, words of destiny and vision, but don't offer help to clean up the mess. When they place demands, calmly set boundaries. Step back so you don't form a one-sided relationship in which the addict is dependent on you and feels no worth or self-esteem. Don't ever give up on your addict, but keep your hands off and your mean words far away. Without being harsh, make some space to get off of the merry-go-round and check your emotional and mental health. This involves saying no, which is one of the most loving things you can do. Sometimes no comes with a lot of pain. Say it anyway.

The enabled live in the same world we live in with the same rules and consequences. But after enough enabling, they're stuck in their role, continually cleaned up after by someone else. They feel incompetent, incapable, dependent, and disempowered. It destroys their self-esteem. Josiah was so intelligent and one of the most handsome human beings I'd ever laid eyes on. Yet he had no self-esteem. He sought acceptance and became dependent on anyone who would offer him a solution to his problems. His own mama, his protector, played the largest role in this, and she called it love.

The enabled person doesn't have to build skills or figure life out. They simply exist and never understand their full potential. Enabling cripples and debilitates them. Because they feel incapable, the enabled person holds their enabler emotionally hostage through forms of manipulation, all in order to keep the pattern going. It's a cycle in which everyone loses.

Thanksgiving of 2012 was hard for all of us. Josiah had moved in with his cousin, his drug use never slowing down. I often texted or called, but I never got a response. The holiday wasn't the same without him, and we all wanted him back. It hurt deep in our hearts. He hadn't had a reason to get sober after constantly being facilitated and enabled. I had picked up all the pieces for him and exhausted every ounce of help I knew. No one stayed at our house long that Thanksgiving. The family seemed to arrive, eat, and promptly leave.

Drugs, yet again, affected the entire family.

The following month was brutal. Josiah was wearing out his welcome where he was staying. He lost his job and stole things in order to buy drugs. All the while, he told everyone he wasn't doing drugs and placed guilt and shame on anyone who asked him if he was. He was a master at manipulation by this point, and he'd counted on it working on me for months. He manipulated his family members into thinking Mom no longer cared or believed in him and that Dad hated and was ashamed of him.

At first, I was upset and hurt when friends and family took him in, providing yet another way for him to stay on drugs. I had stopped enabling my son and naively thought everyone else would too. The day he got caught using in the bathroom where he was living, his cousin had had enough. She kicked him out. He had already used up all his chances with his friends. Now he had done so with his family. I was relieved when others began to see that enabling wasn't helping.

Josiah somehow procured a tent that he set up at the bottom of our property. It was winter—freezing cold in the mornings and at night. Austin went down the hill every day to cut wood for fire. Our broken hearts didn't slow Josiah's drug use. He was slamming a lot of dope. My nephew worried that he wouldn't be satisfied taking only enough heroin to get high. He was afraid Josiah might overdose.

Christmas was spent crying all day and evening. We were stifled by the weight of sorrow and pain. Montana took a plate of holiday food to Josiah's tent. I couldn't celebrate when my son was in that kind of shape. I cried and cried. I experienced the deepest sorrow I'd ever felt. My whole body felt sick. A heavy cloud of distress lay over me, pushing on my lungs until I gasped for breath. The hardship lent a melancholy tone to the entire household. My soul was anguished. I couldn't lift myself out of it; it overtook me and snatched my brain away. That whole day, I was only physically present. Mentally, I was completely gone. Another holiday was ruined.

How did we get here? How would it end? I had no answers. I knew I was doing what the experts said was best, but it felt like I was dying inside. I was no longer enabling my son. I could no longer help him by fixing his life. I wasn't providing a way of escape or an easy road that would keep him heading toward death.

Yet the sadness consumed me. I forced myself to believe that not enabling him would help him hit his rock bottom very soon. I had to hold onto that belief. I just didn't know what rock bottom looked like, and I was completely ill-prepared. I had heard "overdose" spoken many times, but it had never taken root in my mind. I suppose I thought that one day he'd wake up cold and filthy, wanting nothing to do with what had gotten him there. Reality wasn't my friend. I avoided it at all costs.

For eighteen years, I had protected and loved my Josiah. Now, my son had tried opiates and gotten hooked. I unwittingly enabled him to kill himself, believing I could save him from this evil intruder.

I had a set way of thinking, one perspective formed by my entire life experience, home and culture, church and community, attitudes and emotions, and personality. If someone tells me the sky is black when I've been certain my whole life it's blue, it would take substantial evidence to convince me to unlearn the color I see when I look up.

My natural propensity as a mom had been to love my children exactly as I had done for years. Until suddenly, I was instructed to switch gears and love differently. It was like being thrown at the age of thirty-nine into a region that only speaks Chinese. I was so overwhelmed by this new language. For the sake of my child, I had to learn it quickly, and I did the best I could. I avoided the old language, worried it would cause me confusion. Still, confusion was inevitable, and it was a brutal process. My set of ideas and beliefs had to be replaced. The language of enabling was so ingrained in me, unlearning it felt abnormal and artificial.

There's a whole spectrum of what people call love. That one word does so much: it motivates us to act and respond, it moves us toward compassion and the desire to help, and it has the power to kill an addict. The family on the merry-go-round goes nowhere. When a child suffers because of what we call love, then we must unlearn.

Educate yourself on healthy love. Stop trying to control your children. Allow them to experience the results of their choices. Don't scream and belittle them, but don't hand them money and pick up their mess. Don't nag them about their responsibilities and supply a place to live while they are killing themselves with drugs. Trust that you don't have to fix this for them.

As I did my part to unlearn my lifelong behavior, I came across stories of parents enabling their children to death. Stories that I could uncannily relate to. I joined a social media page for moms of addicts. It opened my eyes. One 2019 post from the Facebook page M.O.M (Mother's on a Mission) Fighting Against Addiction spoke deeply to my heart:

A love letter to my addicted adult child:

My Dear Child,

I feel like I am saying goodbye to you, and in a way, I suppose I am. I will always love you. I want the very best for you, and I am prepared to do the most unnatural thing a mother can ever do. My mind screams, I'm abandoning you. Oh, I know you're all grown up, but to me, you'll always be my baby. That's part of the problem. My nature is to protect you. I see you broken and despairing, and I am broken and despairing too. If you had cancer or heart disease, I would fight tooth and nail to get you the care you need.

In a strange way, this is me fighting, It's the hardest fight I've ever fought. It would be far easier to stand at your hospital bed, knowing that what I was doing was helping you. But there is no hospital bed, there is no cancer or heart disease. What there is, is an insidious little secret, one that has grown into a horrible, ugly beast; it is devouring you alive and me right along with it.

I've watched this monster grow, I've pleaded with it, I've coddled it, I've even nurtured it. I've done everything I can think of to make this THING go away, but it is relentless. I am left to face the truth. You, my precious child, are an addict.

86

An addict!!! Oh, my God, I can barely say it. I feel sick, I hate that word. And yet, it is true. Why does the truth have to be so hard? Even harder is what I still have to do.

All my life I have watched over you, and now I have to set you free. Not because I want to. Because I need to. It's the only thing I can do that might save your life. But the process may also end it. I'm told by other addicts and professionals, and other moms who have gone before me, there is a far greater chance you will have success and get clean if I do this. Almost always, this works. Believe me, almost is nowhere near comforting enough. If I wasn't sure I was helping you to die, I would never choose this.

But here I am, between a rock and a hard place. With no good choices, only hard and worse ones. Before I let you go, know this, I am here for you always! I am here for YOU! Not for your disease, but the you I know hides deep down inside the addict, somewhere. Whether you get clean by intervention or you grow weary of the consequences now that you are dealing with them, or be it by divine intervention, this insanity will stop.

If you ever thought it might be hard quitting drugs, my dear, you should try walking away from your child. I know we've both grown sick with this monster. You're not the only one who needs help, I do too. I promise you, I'll do everything that is asked of me, even if I hate every minute of it. I'll do it, because I know if I do, you might. I promise not to ask you to do anything that I won't do. I would ask you to take care, but you will only smile and nod, and carry on like before. The words would only make me feel better; they're of no use to you. So instead, I shall give you to God. I don't know who else to trust you with. I'll wrap you in your favorite baby blanket. The one you dragged behind you until it was nothing but rags. I will pray for you and for me. I will pray that we both have the strength to do the next right thing, even when it feels so wrong.

Go with God, my dear sweet child.

May we both find peace.
Love, Mom

TODAY, IT SADDENS ME that these groups are private. The general public can be so judgmental toward addicts, forcing the suffering families of addicts into privacy. I refuse to keep my struggles and my addict private. I don't care what people think or say. I shout it from the rooftops: my life is about helping others, and I can't help if I am not willing to expose my life. We are all part of its vicious cycle. We must open our eyes to this reality.

Are you loving your addict to death? It's one of the toughest questions I had to ask myself, but also the most necessary. My self-esteem has been dependent on my ability and willingness to help, which becomes a harmful characteristic when it involves "helping" in inappropriate ways. I falsely felt in control when the situation was one that couldn't be controlled, and the attempts to control ultimately made the situation worse. Stepping in to solve my children's problems diminishes their motivation to cope and act responsibly. Without any motivation, there is little incentive for change. Enablers help the enabled dig deeper into dysfunctional living. I helped my son dig his own grave.

CHAPTER 8
Abandoned by God

MY MIND WAS RACING at a pace I couldn't process. I burst through the doors of the Emergency Room, scanning the room for clues of where to go. The looks on the faces around me said it all. A nurse rushed to my side and told me what had happened. Josiah had been dropped off curbside with no pulse or signs of life. They'd administered Narcan, and the doctors were working on him. I rounded the corner to a room full of medical staff huddled around a bed; a man in the center was administering chest compressions. Their facial expressions were full of concern, eyebrows knitted in deep, targeted concentration. A beehive of indistinguishable white coats, each one took turns administering the next antidote like a bee going in for nectar before flying back to repeat the cycle over and over.

A plethora of feelings circulated through me. One moment I was unable to feel my body, the next my heart and mind sprung to action, and I found myself crying and gasping for breath before succumbing again to numbness in a maddening and unstoppable free fall.

The doctors encircling his bed kept working on Josiah. In what was probably a few minutes but seemed like ages, there was an outcry. "We got a pulse!" Adrenaline poured into my heart. Still gravely concerned, I hung onto these words. "They got a pulse?" I repeated. The attending doctors stopped what they were doing and watched. The staff wouldn't allow us in the emergency bay, but we could stay close by in an adjacent hallway. We didn't utter a word, standing motionless as we watched them tending steadfastly to Josiah's lifeless body. The doctor periodically shouted for prescriptions, one of the white coats stepping in each time to dispense what had been ordered. All the while, I pulsed with a ceaseless excess of emotion.

Some time later, the doctor made his way over to me and Jason. He told us that if Josiah survived—and it was a slim chance—he'd only do so with severe brain damage, likely unable ever to walk or talk again. The words hung in the air, scrolling through my mind over and over. He said Josiah had overdosed on heroin and was left for dead on the hospital curb. The staff spotted him through their cameras and responded, but he was unconscious, already purple, by the time they'd gotten to him. The doctor estimated he'd gone five minutes without oxygen.

Hearing that was a sucker punch that took my breath away. I began to hyperventilate, pained and panicked to my very soul. I had served God with all my heart, had given Him my all. I had done everything people had advised. I had even let go of Josiah and placed him in God's hands. I had trusted God to quickly help Josiah get free from drugs. I was His faithful servant, the one who believed God would heal my son from addiction. I hadn't wavered from my belief. Not until that moment. Then, I allowed the enemy to enter my mind and snatch me away.

I was instantly mad. Mad at God, mad at the girlfriend he'd been with, mad at the drug friends. I was so mad that I checked out emotionally and psychologically. I was done with God. I wasn't going to give him my prized possession ever again.

Drugs had taken their toll on me. I was tired and worn out, devoid of spirit. I felt abandoned by God. The girl with big faith was left with none. I thought my faith in Him would make the consequences of my son's actions null and void. My brain was twisted. Much like Josiah, I had faith in a God I had fashioned in the image of me. I had made God out to be an enabler and formed Him in my mind to want what I wanted. I wanted His actions to control my son and keep him from killing himself. I didn't understand or realize at the time the many ways in which God was, in fact, teaching me about who He really is.

For the first twenty years of my life, I had viewed

God as a dictator. When I had thought I'd freed my mind from that belief, I went all the way to the other side, deciding He was like me. He would save me and my loved ones, no matter what any of us did. Having faith meant I controlled Him to do what I wanted.

Yet, God gives us all free will to choose, and with choice comes consequence. No matter what we do, His love never changes. But sin kills. Drugs are an explicit example of what sin does to a person. Some sins are subtle and gradual, but they all end in the same thing: death. Death of sanity, death of relationships, death of rational thinking, death of jobs and security, death of innocence.... Still, day in and day out, people blame God for the field of death growing in their lives.

Within the next half hour, a nurse came to tell me Josiah was asking for me. I ran, rounding the corner and immediately locking eyes with him. My beautiful boy, practically skin and bones, his face covered in scabs, the look of death written deep in his eyes, saw me. Tears began rolling down his face. "Why didn't they let me die, Mom?" It took all the strength he could muster to ask. "Why did they save me? Why didn't they just let me die?" The tears on my face matched his.

Many years prior to this, when Josiah was a little boy saying his prayers at night, I had a similar question. Everything in my world was upside down. I hated life. I hated myself. Love was beyond me. I wasn't created to be loved by anyone. My life was nothing but pain and anguish. I harbored guilt, shame, fear, and deep sorrow. I inflicted the same agony birthed in my soul onto my family. I wished it would end many times. I begged God to take me. I knew in my heart of hearts I was too far gone to be helped. God had made the biggest mistake, creating me. Little did I know, Josiah's prayers were being answered. Now it was time for me to pray for my Siah.

He had overdosed and was given a slim chance to live and an even slimmer one to survive in any way other than as a paraplegic. The trauma squelched my spirit. I hadn't yet considered that this could happen. I hadn't even entertained the thought of losing my son.

The minute I walked into the hospital, I shut down and checked out. The news was more than my emotional capacity could handle. I was there in body, but I was gone otherwise—psychologically, emotionally, spiritually. I had lost all hope. I went through the motions of life, church, and work, but I was always on autopilot. I lived each day mechanically, knowing what needed to be accomplished for the day but having no heart, drive, or passion in carrying it out. I was living in another dimension; reality was too harsh for me to stay present in.

Josiah, once recovering in the ICU unit, again vowed never to touch a drug. No matter what. He was finished for good. Drugs had turned me cynical and bitter. I no longer believed a single word that came out of his mouth. I was fed up and tired of the hammer that came down on my heart every time I believed him.

Josiah was very perceptive—he knew something was wrong and told me he would go to rehab. The thought of it made me happy, but I didn't count on it. I told him that rehab would at least be a warm bed and food. He could see he was no longer going to be able to manipulate me. He even told me later he feared I had given up on him completely. I can see why he felt that way. For nineteen years, I had loved him one way. Now, everything was different.

> "Whenever our heart condemns us, God is greater than our heart and He knows everything."
> — 1 John 3:20

AFTER DAYS AT THE HOSPITAL, I went home and looked at my house. There wasn't a single thing left of any value. Our garage, once brimming with camping supplies, tools, decorations, and sentimental things, was empty. It seemed so painful and devastating in the moment. In hindsight, it was probably one of the best lessons I could have learned. We spend years filling our homes with things. We use every penny we earn to buy more stuff. We get so wrapped up in what we have monetarily. When it's all taken away, in the moment it feels so violating. It's as if our "stuff" was more sacred to us than our son's life. Josiah was alive, yet there I was, feeling dead.

From day one, I had wanted my son to be free from drugs. No longer did I have an optimistic attitude or a feeling of relief that Josiah was alive. I felt nothing but pain and heartache. I got slammed so hard that I was dazed like a bird who hit a clear window in full-throttle flight. Up until this point, my relationship with God was ignorant. It was built on shifting sand instead of solid rock, blown away by the coming storm. God had to bring me there, to shatter that belief system in order to rebuild a solid, unshakeable foundation for the future. My reign as the god of my life was ending. I would have to build a new house—healthy and structurally sound.

But unlearning is so much harder than learning.

My whole identity was bound up in my role as a mom who picks her children up when they fall. But this was a nightmare that I couldn't control. None of my maternal tools could make it go away. I truly thought that listening to and following the "formula" I'd learned would magically bring back the Josiah we all knew and loved. I knew I was no longer enabling him, but I had yet to fully grasp that this was all Josiah's choice. It was all part of the process of unlearning, which I was tempted to give up on, time and time again.

CHAPTER 9
All Hell Breaks Loose

JOSIAH WAS RELEASED from the hospital, and he was off to Phoenix in no time—right where his heroin addiction had begun.

He would call us periodically asking us to pick up his car while he went to detox. We did. He would go into detox for days and call us to come get him. We did. He would come home clean but soon head back to Phoenix. He even attempted to do heroin again in our house. We would catch him, and he'd run back off to Phoenix. Each time, we spent days cleaning up all the mess, a tornado of paraphernalia scattered throughout our home. Josiah left a path of destruction each time he lived with us.

We did this dance for months, always willing to be a part of his healing. I was told to meet Josiah where he was. If he wants to get well, meet him there, but don't pursue detox or make calls or appointments on his behalf. I had stopped giving him money, but I was still giving him rides. It's all a process of learning what is and isn't enabling.

After the fourth or fifth time he got clean and asked to come home, I started treating him like a toddler again. I made him come to the gym with me during the day and sleep in our room at night. I didn't trust him and I wouldn't let him out of my sight. Our relationship was fraught with broken trust and promises. He'd be in the bathroom for too long, and paranoia would consume my heart and mind. We would walk into a store and I'd fear he'd steal merchandise. With an addict, fear is a constant companion, terrorizing you every day. Every time your addict uses again, your fear materializes. Even in the good moments, I lived every day grieving for my son who wasn't even dead, hopeless he'd ever get off drugs.

Josiah and his girlfriend broke up, severing his ties to Phoenix. But he still went there again and again, and we all knew why.

I hadn't expected to hear from him for a while, as that was his pattern when using, but it only took a matter of days. It was July 2014 and hot as hell. My phone rang. Josiah's name flashed on my phone screen. I always prayed it would be his voice on the other end when I answered. "Mama?" It was him. "Hey, son." I choked back tears and continued, "Where are you?" He told me he was going into a detox center and then rehab. He had lied so many times about rehab, that he had called centers and no one had a bed for him, that no centers would accept him without insurance. I didn't believe this time would be any different, but I expressed to him what I knew to be right, that I knew he'd beat the addiction, even though my heart didn't feel it.

"I'm at the Salvation Army in Tucson. They have a bed for me, but they won't let me leave my car here." "You need me to come get it?" I inquired. "Yeah, let me ask someone for the address." I could hear what the lady said as I jotted down the address. He said they wouldn't check him in until his car was moved. I assured him I'd be there as quickly as I could. Jason dropped everything he was doing at work, hitched on his car trailer, and we left for Tucson. I fully expected to drive to the Salvation Army and either have to take him to another detox or not find him there at all.

We pulled in and there he was, beaming from ear to ear. He told us he'd walked around the premises and that they had weight-lifting equipment, a pool, and a store. He seemed genuinely happy to be there. I had a different reaction, my heart aghast at the sight of the place. The tall fences were topped with barbed wire and the windows were barred. It looked like a prison. We had to ring a buzzer to get through the front door. I couldn't believe this was what it had come to. How could this possibly help my son? I didn't vocalize these thoughts, but Josiah could sense something was wrong. I made light of my attitude and said I wasn't feeling well.

Josiah rang the buzzer and told them who he was.

They opened the door. A man—the gatekeeper—told us we weren't allowed in with Josiah. He told us that after the initial thirty days, Josiah could call us. He motioned for Josiah to come in and shut the door behind him. Just like that. Jason and I stood there for a few moments, paralyzed, numb, heartbroken, relieved...

"Let's go, babes," Jason's voice broke the silence. We rounded the corner toward the car and heard a shout. "Mama, Dad!" Josiah had made his way to the weight room outside to bid us goodbye. He gave us a big wave and a huge smile through the chain-link fence. We went up to the fence and told him how much we loved him and how proud were, sure he'd do great.

I held back the tears until I got in the car and then cried all the way home. I didn't know how to make this pain go away. Watching the door close behind him, knowing he had to be locked up, killed me. Seeing my child taken to a place encased by bars and barbed wire where all the doors are locked ripped my heart open. To think that a substance can take my prized possession to a place like that was incomprehensible. Josiah's freedom was gone, replaced by confinement and imprisonment, bound by other human beings who said this was "help." This wasn't supposed to be my Josiah's life.

A COUPLE WEEKS AFTER Josiah had been in rehab, Jason and I received a certified letter from a Phoenix attorney. We were being sued for one million dollars. A girl suffered a stroke in the gym where I thought I was part owner and was holding Jason's business and us personally responsible.

We consulted an attorney and were assigned tedious and convoluted tasks. For the next month, I was bulldozed into the ground all over again. I couldn't think straight or navigate how this could even be happening. As we procured all the information for our attorney, another situation arose. A coach at the gym was behaving unethically toward the customers. This news arose at the same time as I learned I wasn't technically the owner of the business because I had never been added to it as I had been told.

It was all too heavy. I wanted to check out of reality. I wasn't myself. I was typically the first one at church. I looked forward to our assembly and studied the Bible ferociously. My studies poured so much into me, and I eagerly awaited pouring it all out. I was called to preach and teach and felt alive when I spoke at church—until now. Every weekend, I instead planned intentionally distracting activities, camping or hiking or all-night bonfires—anything I could do to escape. This is how addiction becomes a family disease.

After thirty days, Josiah got to call. The first call went really well, but each one after that was torturous. He'd beg me to come get him. He believed he was healed. I had to refuse him over and over. I could hear in his voice when he was feigning, his words manipulative and cunning once again. My heart wanted to give in but my words never changed. I gradually got better at doing what didn't feel natural—loving in a new way. I was learning to deal with Josiah from a place of understanding as opposed to feeling, but I continued to believe in him and knew he could do it. If he wanted out of there, he could leave and go to prison. It was his choice.

We were allowed to go to church with Josiah after he had spent sixty days at the Salvation Army rehab. After ninety, we got to take him on three-hour outings. By then, he truly seemed back to his old self, though he still complained that his brain didn't function normally and that he battled depression and anxiety. I tried to shelter him from all that was going on in our life, worried it might jeopardize his sobriety. Intense feelings and hardship can provoke drug users to start using again. Josiah was dealing with enough already: shame, identity loss, no job, no car, no possessions at all. I didn't want to emphasize another problem he might feel tempted to clean up. Josiah perceived the distance as me treating him like a stranger. He felt like we viewed him differently, despite our unconditional love for him, which we tried our best to express under the circumstances.

This was the hardest year of my entire life. Everything was completely out of my control. Everything— my son, my valuables, my business, my finances, and my friends—was gone! The bottom had fallen out from under me. I was in an endless free fall.

All hell broke loose, and now we were barely staying afloat financially. Jason didn't have a lot of work and passed by a new metal building that was under construction along the highway. Glancing over, he felt impressed by the Lord to offer his help with the construction. Jason quickly dismissed the impulse. It couldn't be God. After all, we were doing all we could to keep our business going, now well over $30,000 in attorney fees. He passed the metal building again the next day and felt the same calling. This time he told me about it.

They were building a new church in town. I initially thought, "Really? Another dang church?" Our small city seems to have a church on every corner; the last thing we need is one more. Why on earth would the Lord impress Jason to go work on yet another church when we were going through utter hell in our lives? Still, there was a knowing inside of me: God works in mysterious ways; we have to trust His lead. We have had a close relationship with Christ for many years, led and guided by him countless times in our home, marriage, business, and church lives. Having experienced Him in such an intimate way, we know when He speaks into our hearts. I told Jason that feeling the pull two days in a row meant he should probably go and do what he felt called to do.

The contractor instructed him to see the pastor who was at another church until this one was finished.

Jason drove over and offered his services and phone number, the pastor thanking him. Jason came home and told me he'd done what he had been told to do. Neither of us thought about it again.

A couple months passed. In that time, God had begun to work on my heart about moving to a new church. I was resistant; we'd already gone through so much this year. I had attended my "home" church for twenty years; it was where my dad served as pastor. I couldn't imagine where on earth God was sending us, but I couldn't get away from this calling for newness. I entertained the thought of continuing to go to the Salvation Army every Sunday and felt a strong no. Anyway, Josiah would be getting out soon and would need a place of refuge to help him rebuild his life.

During this struggle, Jason got a call from the pastor he met with a couple months prior. Jason was in the middle of a big job, his first in months, but he dropped everything and went to help build the new church. When Jason told me, I felt a drawing in my spirit to go to The River. I had no idea why I was being sent there, but, after several more confirmations, I visited with my mom and dad. I told them I felt the Lord was calling me there, and they both sent us with their blessing.

We attended their Sunday morning service. I cried all the way through. The pastor brought me some books he had written, which I took home and devoured within a week. Gradually, I met people at the church and soon discovered that many of its members were recovering addicts. There turned out to be many success stories in that 1% recovery statistic within those four walls. I finally understood why we were there.

When we first went to The River, Jason and I were a complete mess. We were in the middle of the lawsuit, Jason worked sunup to sundown, and we were nearly bankrupt. I was working long hours running the gym by myself. Knowing Josiah would be getting out of rehab soon was weighing on me. My friends had walked out of my life and created a whirlwind of local drama about me on social media. The pinnacle of this stressful period was a six-hour deposition I'd have to endure, an attorney grilling me and spinning my words into untruths to be used against me. It was torturous and grueling, and I felt alone and afraid, mentally back to square one. I felt pelted by waves of turmoil, unable to come up for air, drowning with zero ability to save myself. I was unable to see tomorrow, terrified of what it might bring. Every single thing in my life was in ashes. Nothing was solid; it was shifting and unstable. I didn't know from day to day what giant, life-altering drama would slam up against me next. Nothing was in my control. With everything I was facing, death seemed so much easier than this intolerable existence.

The deposition left me so empty and drained, I didn't think I could drive myself home. Jason hadn't been allowed to accompany me—he couldn't, even if he'd wanted to. He had to earn money to pay for the attorney. Although the past year had contained an excessive amount of horror, this was the last straw. I don't remember driving home, but somehow I did. I crawled into bed without a single shred of fight left in me. I curled into a ball and begged God to take my life. I burned with fever and horrible body aches, racked by vomiting and chills. I was completely hopeless.

> "The Lord is my rock, my fortress
> and Savior, my God is my rock
> in whom I find protection. He
> is my shield, the strength of my
> salvation and my stronghold."
> — *Psalm* 18:2

AFTER DAYS IN BED, my phone buzzed. I got a text message from my new pastor, whom I hardly knew, asking me what the Lord had shown me over the weekend. I quickly responded, "You don't want to know." I thought I'd hit bottom many times before, but this was a new low. Even so, I knew I couldn't stay in bed forever. Much to my chagrin, I rolled out of bed, sat on my bedroom floor, and demanded: "God, show me something."

A scene flashed through my mind of a happy dog and its owner walking through the woods. I sensed the owner loved his dog very much, and he told him to stay where he was, no matter what. He drew a circle around the dog and told his beloved pet to stay inside the circle, no matter what he heard or saw. He assured his dog he'd be back for him. Then a forest fire, hot and terrifying, was blazing around the dog. The dog trusted the master's love for him and didn't move a muscle. He was willing to go through hell because he trusted his owner.

The dog burned alive, in torturous, excruciating, agonizing pain. I quickly related to the feelings of the dog. It grieved me to my core, and sobs came from deep within me. When the owner returned, all that remained were ashes. As quickly as the pain hit my soul, the dog was reborn in the master. No longer limited to a bark, he now had a voice. No longer low to the ground, he now had legs. He had a sound mind, his life now hidden in his master. He was a brand new being, taking on the form of the master.

God spoke to me: "This is a picture of you. You stayed and endured the torture, and now your life is hidden in Me." The sickness left my body. No longer was I trampled by the deep oppression. I could breathe and see clearly. A new hope was birthed inside of me. I told my pastor and knew, in that moment, I was right where God had planted me.

To be hidden in Christ, the old me who couldn't handle life and its many agonizing moments, who couldn't force my son to be sober no matter how I tried, had to die. A whole new world opened up to me. I wasn't God of this world, but I got to enjoy all its benefits. This world offered peace instead of turmoil, unconditional love instead of love built in my image. I saw myself through a new set of eyes, free from the weight of the many uncontrollable circumstances I was in. I would have another chance to trust God with my son. I didn't know when or how, but I knew.

I started from ground zero. I had been in ministry for many years, but I was now at a brand new church with no one who knew me or where I'd come from. I didn't minister; I just sat in a pew for the very first time in my life. I felt like a brand new Christian, struggling to understand the preacher. Bits and pieces pierced into my soul, and I cried at each and every service. My new pastor preached so differently from my dad.

It was a hard time for me. Not only was I in a new place with new people, but I was also learning a new God. The real God verses the god I had created in my own image—an enabling god on one hand and a judge ready to crush me on the other. I began to learn the love of the Father. I was now placed in a church with a healthy culture and a perspective of God that was completely foreign to me. I felt inadequate and vulnerable and my heart was fully exposed and raw. I was an open book and didn't feel I should be otherwise, even with strangers. The entire process unraveled me completely. I relearned everything, the epic amount of bullshit and mis-programming I'd been taught my entire life.

I now understood the many ways I still enabled my son. Before I could choose to handle circumstances differently, I had to hit rock bottom. I had read plenty about enabling, but, much like an addict, I had to come to the end for myself. Healthy relationships place loved ones in control of their own lives and place us in a secondary role. The enabler has to return responsibility to the person it truly belongs to. I had to stop taking responsibility for my son's actions. I failed at this multiple times, for doing so required changing who I was at my core.

Looking back, I wouldn't change a thing. It took all of that—drowning, being buried—to comprehend that I was actually being planted, soon to grow into a tall oak tree. Rock bottom had built a new me. I had no more desire to try to control anything. I knew I couldn't.

CHAPTER 10
Ground Zero

JOSIAH GOT OUT OF REHAB a few months after we started at our new church. He seemed to have a new lease on life. He spoke of his future for the first time in a long time. He had big dreams and always reached for the stars. Even now, he believed he could lasso the moon.

Back home, Josiah started working for his dad. Meanwhile, I was miserable, but for once it was unrelated to him. Instead, I was dealing with near bankruptcy, lost relationships, and countless hours of work, as well as the lingering pain of gossip and drama. My mind was wrapped up in myself and rebuilding my life.

Josiah asked me to save his checks, minus cigarettes and food, and only give him money as he needed it. He had probation and fines to pay off. For a few months, he was doing really well, and I believed the addiction chapter was behind us.

He would travel once more to Phoenix to party with his old friends. Josiah loved a party. He kept his checks and took the money I'd been saving for him. He started going to raves, telling me later that he'd done ecstasy. He reasoned that "it wasn't heroin." For an addict, one is too many and a thousand is not enough.

At a college party in Phoenix, Josiah met the love of his life: a bombshell foreigner, blonde, educated, and sophisticated. She would later recall all the girls at the party telling her that any guy there was suitable, just not Josiah. "Stay away from Josiah," they'd say. Josiah was a ladies' man, and the girls wanted to protect this beautiful foreigner.

In no time, the two were inseparable. For five months, it was all fun and parties. He would come home and work during the week and go off to party on the weekends. We knew he was playing with fire, but we didn't know he was already burning.

His romance in full bloom, Josiah was traveling to Phoenix as much as he could, coming back home during the week for work, first on Monday mornings, then on Tuesdays, until eventually he wasn't showing up until Wednesdays. It was nearing the end of the semester, and they were partying hard. Josiah was active on social media, and we got to watch his crazy weekend adventures unfolding. The parties made me uneasy. I feared danger was ahead.

Josiah learned to hide his addiction from me pretty well. He would only use the bare minimum during the day and still be up and active. The only physical signs were the scabs on his face. He had gained a little weight and started lifting again, and he seemed to be functioning relatively normally.

The possibility that he could still be using always nagged at the back of my mind, a constant gnawing in my soul that I would push back. Ignorance is bliss, and I have a natural tendency to believe people to a fault.

I saw signs but didn't accept them and excused them from my mind. I didn't want to believe them. I don't know where he was shooting up because his arms were clear. We have veins all over our bodies, and addicts learn to hide the marks remarkably well. Several events were dead giveaways: blood all over the bathroom floor of our hotel on a trip to Texas, allegedly the result of his girlfriend's nosebleed; loud snoring and a hoarse voice; constant anger and belligerence. His inner light began dimming again, his eyes no longer wide open or alert. With everything going on in my life, I pushed down the suspicions, wanting them to be untrue because it was too painful to admit, and I didn't know if I could handle any more. But addiction can't hide long before it manifests outwardly.

In May of 2015, Josiah relapsed on heroin. I wasn't immediately aware, but I was constantly cautioning him to be careful about who he hung out with. His probation officer was also suspicious he had spiraled. He was being mean and lashing out at his girlfriend.

I found evidence he'd tried to break into my car. Despite this, I never stopped trying to speak life into my son. I believed I had words of love and could reason with him so that he would trust me and get himself help. I sat him down in the living room and told him that he'd soon be violating probation and couldn't live in our house and do drugs.

This time, he told me he'd get himself to rehab. He didn't do his normal song and dance about being sober. His girlfriend was days away from going back to France, and he knew his future was with her. He loved her and didn't want to lose her. He had a buddy who had successfully completed the Phoenix Rescue Mission and stayed on after as a mentor. Josiah messaged him and asked if they had a bed available. It took a couple hours, then the friend called and said he was in.

We loaded up and headed for Phoenix—Josiah, his girlfriend, and me. They don't allow you to go into any program with any amount of drugs in your system, which is why people go to detox before rehab. The Phoenix Rescue Mission had a homeless shelter where Josiah would detox, in filthy living conditions, with no beds, surrounded by hundreds of homeless people who were dope sick and racked by pain. This wasn't my first time dropping my son off at a facility, but it was his girlfriend's. We said our goodbyes as she sobbed. The sight of him walking through the gates and disappearing into a mass of homeless people is burned into my memory. It was a scene straight out of a nightmare.

On the long rides home from taking him all over the state of Arizona, I often asked myself how we got here and how we could get out. Jason and I may have jumped off the merry-go-round, but each time we dropped Josiah off, it felt like a piece of our hearts was torn to shreds. It's amazing how we would grieve the living over and over and over. Each time Josiah chose to slam dope, we felt the agony of that. As much as we love, we grieve. The soul's anguish seems more than a human can bear, harassing us day and night. Grief is the love we want to give, but can't. Watching our son choose a substance that was slowly killing him, unable to stop it, felt like a knife to the heart.

Drug abuse makes pain a constant in your life. The pain defines who you are: either the victim or the victor. Your addict needs you to be the latter, to grow from the pain, with more courage and drive than you ever had before it. That helps the addict use his pain to grow once he's hit rock bottom. If you let your pain victimize you, your addict will follow suit, wallowing in it, running from it, and pushing it away. One step at a time, allow the pain to integrate into and be useful for your life. Pain is the boat to get you across the water. You make the choice to get in it and trust it will take you somewhere safe and not let you drown.

> "Finding meaning in your pain involves asking yourself who you want to be as a result of your grief."
>
> — *Sameet Kumar*

JOSIAH FLOURISHED at the Phoenix Rescue Mission. He was in a smaller unit with fewer addicts who got more individual time with their mentor. He called his mentor his own "personal pastor." Josiah grew to love this man, who poured hope and visions into his future. He was also a recovering addict who used his failures and mistakes to make a solid difference in the lives of these struggling young men.

One day, Josiah called me and said he'd asked to be baptized. Drugs had taken Josiah's faith and flushed it down the toilet. He had questioned if there even was a God. After the initial shock, I was elated and filled with hope. He told me everything he'd learned and about the tools he'd been given for when life's pressures hit him. On October 7, 2015, he was baptized. For the first time, he was aware and honest in saying he couldn't beat this on his own and required help.

Even if we aren't addicted to heroin, many of us know what it's like to believe we don't need help and can do things on our own.

Our family as a whole seemed to be getting healthier. We learned to identify dysfunction and actively pursued healthy practices of thinking and loving. We learned that a day sober is a day to celebrate, not to worry. We learned we could be Josiah's biggest fans and not be completely devastated if he faltered. We had to unlearn and relearn how to love and how to talk to Josiah. We understood that each time he got out of rehab, Josiah would feel like a stranger coming home. We worked hard on our words to him, but it wasn't easy.

Completely in love and wanting to spend the rest of his life with his girlfriend, Josiah had the challenge he needed to stay in the program and finish strong. She was waiting for him to come to Paris once he'd taken care of things and had the green light to go. He had over a thousand dollars to pay for probation. He had to get a passport and apply for a work visa. He didn't have any friends he could stay with while he looked for a job, so he had to come back to Safford and work for his dad. He had a goal in front of him and wouldn't let anything stop him. He asked me to hold every penny he made so he could take care of all his responsibilities. He asked his dad for overtime hours, working and saving and working and saving. Jason told Josiah we'd buy him a one-way ticket if he could pay off all his debt and get a passport. There was light at the end of the tunnel. This was the Josiah we all knew, driven and thriving at life once again.

There would be multiple hurdles he still had to face, but one by one, he took them all on. He paid off his probation, but he still needed a judge to sign off on his leaving the country. The first few people we talked to said it would take months of processing and getting a passport. Josiah didn't take that answer as gospel. He asked me to take him to the courthouse and went in alone. One week later, he had the green light to leave for Paris. Months after getting out of rehab, Josiah had accomplished his goal and was off to start his new life in Paris. On November 3rd, he left Arizona.

CHAPTER 11
Falling From a Fairytale

A NEW COUNTRY, A FOREIGN LANGUAGE, a different culture, no friends. This was Josiah's new reality. He was head over heels in love, motivated to start a brand new life. He fell in love with Paris too—the culture, the city life, and the language. He wasn't able to procure a work visa in the States, so he had to apply quickly or be sent back. He and his girlfriend applied, called, and visited every embassy in Paris, hitting a dead end at every turn. They decided the only way he could stay would be to get married. On December 16th, Josiah asked Lauren to marry him. She said yes.

What a beautiful romance. From all outward appearances, they were the perfect couple, living the dream. They set a date for the wedding in February of the following year. The wedding was simple, yet sophisticated, chic, and refined. Lauren had a timeless elegance about her, one of the most beautiful brides I'd ever seen. She beamed with happiness from inside.

The wedding was held in an old, historic building with white stone exteriors and wooden flooring. Lauren descended the steps, a picture from an enchanted fairy tale, a modern-day Cinderella. The air outside was crisp, a light wind stirring up leaves and blowing flowers from nearby bushes. The minister was in a full white gown with gold tassels and a long strip of white cloth around his neck, a large book in hand.

The ceremony was conducted in French and translated into English. It was romantic, poetic, and intimate, surrounded by the people they cherished most. I allowed my mind to wander a bit, thinking about all the events that had led up to this day. What a roller-coaster ride, what a mind-blowing finish. It was a perfect day, so I resigned to let everything from the years prior tuck neatly away inside of me. This was a new season, a season of beginnings and bright futures. Josiah had overcome his demons and was among the 1% of the world's statistics. He was a fighter, and he'd taken on the worst possible thing that could touch him. He was soon to be a husband, and one day, I hoped, a father.

The ceremony concluded with an effortless, modest meeting of lips and the pronunciation of Mr. and Mrs. Josiah Kouts. Tears of joy ran down my cheeks and elation filled my heart. We adjourned to Lauren's family's home. The table was set with white linen, a bouquet of flowers in the center. Candles were lit throughout the room and the smell of homemade food filled our senses. What amazing customs the French have as far as eating and celebrating!

The mother of the bride had prepared course upon course of delectable food, complete with wine and champagne. For hours, we sat and ate. We told stories, laughing and drinking wine, which goes down like juice in France. The hours flew by as we enjoyed every last second together. At the end of the day, I reflected on it as the best I'd had in many years. The following days were much the same. Our new family spent countless hours with us and gave us tours of the most incredible sights I had ever laid my eyes on. It was a trip I'll forever hold close to my heart. For a moment, all was well in the world.

Goodbyes are always hard—even more so when your kid lives in another country and visits will be few and far between. Josiah and I both cried and felt deep sorrow that we'd be apart from each other in our day-to-day lives. As excited as I was for him to have his own family and make a life for them, it was the close of a chapter for the family we had known for twenty-three years. I had gained an amazing daughter and was given such peace knowing my son was with a woman who loved him unconditionally. The comforting thought made it a bit more bearable that he lived a world away from us.

Walking away from him at the airport, I kept looking back—so did he—and saw the pain in his eyes and the tears rolling down his cheeks. He loved his family and his mama. It was a brand new reality we both had to swallow. I had to remind myself over and over that everything works out the way it's meant to.

In the months following the wedding, I was treated to some of the greatest calls I'd ever received as a mother. My son and daughter-in-law were happy and adventurous, the two fitting together like peanut butter and jelly. They both needed little sleep and lived in a city full of excitement and exploration. Josiah would tell me the details of all their new adventures with his characteristic flair for words. He had a fondness for city life, he told me over and over. He and his new bride completed each other.

A year in, Lauren was working her new job, and Josiah still had not been able to find one, sitting day after day in their flat in Paris. He didn't know anybody and didn't speak the language. Lauren was the new girl at work and put in long hours. With her intelligence, drive, and tenacity, she was sure to work her way up the ladder in no time. Josiah was left in a precarious position. He was bored out of his mind, playing PlayStation all day long and even into the night, hours after Lauren would return home.

Addiction isn't just to drugs. If you don't heal your mind, it rears its ugly head in a number of vices. They had fights, either because he felt Lauren was gone too many hours or because he wanted to do whatever he wanted while still trying to control what Lauren did. Lauren would go to business dinners or on business trips and he'd get upset. The long hours spent alone became unbearable. When he first got to Paris, I assured him it wouldn't be forever, maybe a year. A year is a long time to sit and stare at white walls.

France would require him to learn its language, which was good for his mind anyway. But he'd drag his feet with lack of motivation. He missed home and his family, but he loved Paris. His emotions were a wreck. After some months, he knew enough of the language to venture out and order food by himself. Lauren was good for him, making him order in French when they were together. She didn't enable him, and it taught him well.

On the occasions they went out to party, Josiah would go to the pharmacy and look for hangover remedies. In France, low-grade narcotics are sold over the counter. Before long, he was buying boxes and taking their entire contents at once. Coming down from a narcotic, the user gets agitated and mean. He started to withdraw from Lauren and treat her rudely, picking fights more and more.

He managed to hide his use from Lauren for a while, but then she caught on. I got a phone call from her explaining what was going on. I had multiple conversations with Josiah about his addiction. He would start off by swearing he'd only taken the pills to help his hangover, but he always told me the truth eventually. He'd go short periods of time clean before slipping back and letting the addiction take over.

Lauren was going to church and hoping Josiah might join. She would fill me in on the wonderful services and great messages. Josiah refused to go and withdrew only further. Anytime Josiah wasn't sober, he wanted nothing to do with church, even reacting aggressively to the institution. It would have been the perfect opportunity to build his marriage on a solid foundation, but he refused it, spending yet another day of the week in solitude.

Soon enough, he was a full-on addict again. He pushed his wife away and ignored my calls. But he was quickly fed up with the addiction that threatened to cost him everything again. He sought help and was prescribed Suboxone—again. The world's way of helping is to treat an open gash with a bandaid. His moods fluctuated, though anger was his most prevalent. He attempted to control every move Lauren made. When she was home, he was withdrawn and sullen, saying horrible, cutting words. He would call Lauren home from business trips because he'd abused the Suboxone and taken way too much. She would rush home and take him into the doctor.

It was a Sunday morning, and I was busy with my church responsibilities when I got a call from France. I excused myself, on high alert, knowing what Josiah was on and the effect it had on him. It was a hospital in Paris. Josiah had tried to hang himself.

Jason made his way to me because he saw I was visibly shaken. I fell into his arms and sobbed. It attracted a crowd and, before I knew it, I was surrounded by people praying for me. Jason offered to get me on the next plane to France, but I refused it. I couldn't jump in to save him anymore. He had to fight for his own life. He had to learn where drugs took his mind and reap the consequences of his decisions. I was learning this new language of love.

I visited with Josiah when he was able to talk and spoke as much life and destiny as I could muster. He asked me to come to Paris, and I told him I couldn't. I gave him one of my life verses that has proven itself many times. Psalm 34:18 says, "The Lord is close to the brokenhearted; He rescues those who are crushed in spirit." I told Josiah that God was standing ready to deflect the bullets of condemnation and wanted him to run to His safe and loving arms. When I ended the call, I sobbed uncontrollably.

Attempting to live life without healing your mind is like stepping off a ledge. Falling is imminent. Josiah loved a good party. Even more than that, he loved to escape. He loved to be numb and withdrawn from the pressures of life. He wanted to be loved, but he didn't love himself, so he treated anyone close to his heart the way he treated himself. His identity was attained through a false source, threatening to crumble. Though Josiah had watched his parents overcome many obstacles and change in many ways, and as much as he loved a challenge, he succumbed when his whole world was falling apart. Instead of learning healthy coping methods, he repeated the same behavior over and over. It's insanity to do the same thing over and over and expect a different result. Maybe a lot of us are a bit insane.

When his marriage ended, Josiah spent a few months sleeping on the floor of a tiny room with one of his buddies. He wanted to stay in Paris, but he wasn't responsible enough to hold down a job. He spent several cold nights sleeping in the park, where his heart was ignited with compassion for the homeless. He poured out his heart in social media posts about homeless and immigrant people.

Now sober and homeless, he lasted in Paris as long as he could. He'd been on his own since July of 2018 and had just enough money saved to buy a one-way ticket home. Jason and I picked him up from the airport on October 13th—nearly two years after he had left. Though he was heartbroken and his life in disarray, he was sober and thinking clearly. Life in Paris had changed him so much. He was an adult now. He no longer expected me and Jason to do anything for him. He had a plan to come home, work for his dad, and, once again, save every penny so he could return to Paris. First, though, he and his Paris buddies were going on a month-long road trip across the United States.

After three months of saving and planning, the three friends would be setting off on the adventure of a lifetime. Josiah looked better than he had in many years. He had gained a ton of weight and muscle. He was back to the beautiful boy he had been his whole life. He'd go on a few dates but come home disinterested. They weren't Lauren. No one would compare to the love of his life. He made it through the worst heartbreak of his life—sober.

I often said, "Paris grew you up, son." I meant it. He spoke frequently about his demons, his broken heart, and beating his addiction. He struggled constantly with learning to enjoy day-to-day life and trying to stay out of his head. He talked about depression and anxiety, which he hadn't done the entire time he was on drugs. He was finally processing everything he had buried for so long. He felt better than he had in years and wanted sobriety for himself. For the first time in a long time, my soul felt the ease of knowing that drugs were a part of his past. My fear had vanished, replaced by hope in the very core of my soul.

He and his friends would spend New Year's Eve in New York and then split the month up between Chicago, Colorado, Vegas, and California, before heading back to Arizona. It was such an exciting time for Josiah, spent with the people closest to him. They broadcast the trip on social media, and we all got to live vicariously through them at each step. Josiah called me each day while driving to the next city. He would tell me how responsible Moritz was and how crazy fun and unpredictable Mike was. He was somewhere right in between. When they got back to Arizona, they packed up our suburban and headed up the mountain. They were carefree and filled with fun and adventure.

It broke my heart to see these two friends of Josiah's leave. I had just met them, but I already felt like I had known them forever and saw the positive impact they had on my son. The night they left, Josiah's social media post said it all: "One of the biggest mistakes I ever made was watching you guys as you walked away."

Josiah didn't make it to work the next day. When he finally rolled out of bed, he told me he was exhausted from a month of no sleep. He went into the kitchen and made his favorite chorizo and egg burrito before joining his sister, Montana, and me on the couch. Montana handed him her five-month-old baby, Aurora. He played with her for a few minutes and handed her back. He was coughing, sneezing, and blowing his nose and didn't want to get her sick.

Sitting with us, he told us all about his trip. He laughed and told us the quirks each friend had and the funny things each of them did and said. He didn't seem sad. He didn't seem anything but calm, and a bit sick. He told us the three friends had already made a plan to go on another adventure and said he was going to start saving again. My heart was so happy to hear him talk about the future. I always knew my Josiah would be a world changer. He had greatness in him.

CHAPTER 12

Last Dance With the Devil

I WOKE UP THE NEXT MORNING and was out the door by 5:55 to head to church for prayer. After that, I went to the gym to teach my Zumba class, then home to shower and get ready for the day. I got to my morning pastors' meeting, picking up my granddaughter, Aurora, right after to meet Jason for lunch. After lunch, Aurora and I headed to Walmart, then back to church for an afternoon class. I lay Aurora in her car seat as she slept through the entire thing. As soon as it was over, I headed home, Aurora still asleep in her seat. It had been a busy day, and I was hungry for an afternoon snack of tomato and cheese.

Jason got home at 3:45 and said Josiah hadn't shown up for work again. I told him he was sick and suggested he go check on him. I kept cutting tomatoes as I heard Jason go up the wooden steps. I heard him knock on Josiah's door. Getting no answer, he called his name. "Josiah?" I heard him open the hallway door that connects a vanity room to Josiah's bathroom. He knocked and called his name again, now raising his voice, "Josiah!" Austin came out of his room to see what all the commotion was about.

Then I heard Jason speak words I will never forget. "Josiah is dead!" Austin ran to Josiah's room where Jason was screaming uncontrollably. Meanwhile, I walked around in a small circle in the kitchen, over and over, completely in shock.

Jason screamed, "Maria! Call 911, now!" I was jarred back into reality. I came to my senses and flew up the stairs to his room. He was lying on the floor beside his bed, one knee bent, his head almost hidden under the bed skirt. I collapsed onto him and immediately felt his stiff, cold body. His face came into view. It was grey and purple and black, his mouth gaping open, foam excreting and still bubbling out of it. Blood was running out of his eyes and ears, his skin blotched with red. I lay on top of him and pleaded with him as if he could hear me: "No, son. No, baby boy. Why, son?" My entire being was racked with pain that far surpassed anything I'd ever felt in my life. My beautiful boy lay stiff on his bedroom floor, no life left in his young, vibrant being.

Screams filled the house. Austin and Jason were screaming. Jason was running in and out of the house, calling people, screaming "My baby is dead!" at the phone. I barely registered what was happening. Doors were opening and closing. With all the commotion,

Jason's mom came running over from her house next door and sat on the other side of Josiah. I was still lying on him, pleading with him. She began pleading with me. I don't know what a natural response to death is, but perhaps it's that.

Montana was considering becoming a police officer and out on a trial run that afternoon to see what the job would entail. A call came in over the radio. She heard the address and description. The first call Montana got was for her own brother.

They weren't far and made it to our house quickly. I don't know why I allowed him to, but an officer removed me from Josiah's room. I'll forever regret that I didn't refuse to leave the room. It was my son! I had carried him in me for nine months. I had raised him, nursed him, trained him to walk and talk. I had every right to be with him as long as he was in our house. I wanted to be the one to put him in the body bag, not a stranger. I had gone through hell on earth with my son. I wanted to sit by and touch him as long as possible, even in death. I am his mama. I should have that right. I had earned that much. I wanted to be a part of the entire process of his life. I wanted to be present to all of it.

As my family ran and screamed and chased up and down the stairs in panic, I sat outside Josiah's room. I had been sure he had beat it for good. I hadn't been one bit worried or scared. The fear had left me long ago. Despite everything we had been through, he was thriving and had goals and plans for his future. He had walked through hell in the months prior without turning to drugs.

One weak moment, one bad choice, one fatal decision. Josiah had danced with the devil one last time, and the devil doesn't play fair.

Josiah's room swarmed with officers for what seemed like an eternity. My kids and husband were vulnerable and emotionally raw. I attempted to console Austin and Montana, by now twenty-one and twenty-three years old, their pain turning to rage. I held Austin with all my might as I once had Josiah. He was riddled with pain and didn't know what to do with it. We were all dealing with the most intense agony we'd ever experienced, our home taken over by people we barely knew.

> "Jesus came to seek and save
> the lost."
> — Luke 19:10

THE AFTERMATH WAS UGLY. Death left a gaping hole in my heart. It's a suffering so intense that it took over my capacity for rational thought and action. The picture of Josiah's dead body, forever etched in our minds, is a picture of the end game of drug addiction.

Now there were four. Four completely broken people, hearts shattered into a million pieces. A family ripped at the core. What would become of us? I honestly didn't know. I didn't know if I could continue breathing, much less living.

In that moment, I looked for hope that I couldn't see and certainly couldn't feel. I asked Jason over and over if it was going to be okay. Going through such pain, I felt like the only one who has ever experienced it. I didn't know if I could continue living, the intensity of the agony consuming my whole being. Our family looked at one another and saw only deep torment in each other's eyes.

For the first week after Josiah died, I had uncontrollable anxiety attacks and sleepless nights. It had come so unexpectedly, knocking our feet out from under us. We thought Josiah had overcome what should have killed him so many times. We no longer felt like we had sure footing. Everything we knew and thought and believed had been ripped away in a single instant just when we'd thought it was all behind us. He had been on the brink of death over and over without succumbing to losing everything he held so dear. He had remained hopeful and worked hard for his future. His laugh had returned to normal. He had been thriving and striving to reach his dreams and goals once again.

An ache lay heavy over our souls. So many questions left unanswered. There had been no preparing for this. The sting of it, indescribable. It hurt in every part of our bodies.

CHAPTER 13

Broken Together

THE NIGHT JOSIAH DIED, sitting in the loft near his room, I heard the men in his room. They were speaking unintelligibly, walking around and snapping pictures. I wanted to be inside his room with him, putting him on the gurney and zipping up the bag. He was my son. It shouldn't have been strangers who spent the final moments with Josiah.

As I sat there unable to enter, I heard, "Hope is the anchor for your soul." It spoke directly to my crushed soul and rolled over and over in my mind like a powerful, billowing sea. I called Jason over to me and told him what I'd heard. His eyes scanned back and forth from one of my eyes to the other. In the moments following a loss of this magnitude, I deeply sought any inkling of hope to ease the agony in my soul. Little did I know, that little statement would be my beam, my lighthouse in the fiercest storm.

Many people asked me what my experience was like

and if it's "normal" to have a range of emotions that go all over the place when going through something like this. In the months following Josiah's death, I kept a blog, a timeline of my grieving process to help other mama's and families understand that there is no right or wrong way to feel when grief slams up against your life. It's normal to feel all of it!

Blog post: March 23, 2019

Grief is a bitch. I feel like all the hounds of hell are on top of me, and I'm powerless over them. They play on every insecurity within me. I want to hide from everyone around me because I cannot be trusted in the middle of this attack. I can't even navigate through all the bullshit in my brain. The hounds feed me any and all poison, and I feel as if I have no choice but to drink it. I'm so hurt that I don't want to open my mouth in fear that I may hurt everyone that I love. I want to run away and build sky-high walls so the demons can't get out, but I know if I do, there's no chance for light to get in. I have fought so hard to get to where I am today: to be trusted by God and be trusted by those closest to me.

Why are my emotions so strong that it feels like I'm back to square one? I know my feelings are horrific, but I can't change them on my own. Please, God, I beg You, help me walk out of them and not barricade myself behind this state of mind. Help me with this anguish of the soul. The emotions are crushing me; I can't breathe. Can anybody see me? God, I pray not;

but my heart also prays that somebody who won't walk out on me, will see me, and have hope for me when I have none.

If it wouldn't let you down, God, I would take myself out and be with You and Josiah. What's my purpose for staying here? I can't even help myself! I don't feel sorry for myself; I feel bitter anguish in my soul. Until these hounds of hell are gone, I'm going to keep filling my mind with Your Word. I'm going to continue showing up for prayer, even though I cannot utter two words to You. You are God, and I am yours...ALL Yours. Do with me as You please. I have no fight left in me; it died with Josiah. I'm just going on the Word I have hidden inside of me. You won't ever leave me or forsake me, even in the pit of hell, where I am right now. You are with me.

Blog post: March 28, 2019
I don't believe I have ever been as depressed before now. My feelings are in utter darkness, and I'm alone and terrified. I'm calling out to God, yet feeling all alone; it's dragging my mind to the depths of hell. I have zero desire to live. I have zero desire to do anything. This is by far the scariest place I've ever been. I can't think my way out; it's become a part of me for which I never asked. This cannot be the new normal. I won't survive long if it is. I feel like everything I have worked so hard to overcome has been taken away in an instant.

God, please tell me what I've done to hurt You. Why are you allowing me to remain in this desolate place? I will do anything to get out of here! I hate sharing this with Jason. I don't want to discourage him in any way. But I have NO ONE! God, you're out of my reach; I can't see or feel You! Please come to me. Your lap is what I need, Your arms around me and Your whisper in my ear.

Have I completely lost my mind? Will You return it to me? I genuinely hate this place I am in, yet I have no choice in the matter other than to feel it and be with it. Can't my world just end? I tell myself over and over again that joy comes in the morning, then I wake to it not being this morning. I wish joy would run to me now! Save me from these feelings; they are too heavy. Save me from the pounding emotions that are running roughshod over my whole life.

I am not my own Jesus; I belong to You. Deliver me from this pit. Please don't leave me here. I know Josiah is now perfect with a perfect mind. I wouldn't bring him back here to earth. I don't blame You for anything. In fact, I praise You for Your mercy running to my son and setting him free and welcoming him home. So why...why am I in this pit of despair?

Blog post: March 31, 2019
PTSD just kicked into high gear. It affects me and shuts me down in every way. I feel paralyzed to move. I feel frightened and stressed. The images in my mind

flash over and over of Josiah trying to breathe and not being able to as opiates shut down his heart. I know he wasn't awake when he died, but I cannot convince my mind to think that way. What if he was calling for me? Oh, my God, what if he died and he was terrified because he felt like he was drowning? My stomach hurts so bad; anxiety mixed with anguish sits right square in the middle of my gut. I cannot go out into public ever again. I don't want to see people. I want to hide in my closet. I sit and look at the walls and think there is so much I need to be doing, but I'm so exhausted because I no longer sleep. I can't slow my brain even for a few minutes. God, help me, please! Slow my racing heart. Hide me in the cleft of the rock, under Your safe and mighty arms. Ease my heart and emotions in my new "normal" way of life. God, tell my heart to beat normally again.

THIS WENT ON, ENTRY UPON ENTRY, some too explicit to copy. The hardest thing is to accept my emotions while walking through the stages of grief. It feels like sheer torment, the suffering so intense that I often feel it will kill me and fear it won't.

They say grief is love that has nowhere to go. I understood that I had to find a place to channel the pain and give it a place to be released. I used my pain as fuel to ignite the purpose in which I'd been created. Now, all of heaven was cheering me on waiting for me to loose all that can be loosed.

Time passes and the world keeps moving forward. I have some good days. I sense a reprieve from the constant nightmare of my new reality. Then I awaken the next day caught in the clutches of hell all over again. It's a cycle I can't seem to escape. I escape momentarily, only to be chased down another day.

A natural reaction to trauma is to curl up into an emotional ball and forget that I have a family experiencing the same pain. It's too easy to withdraw, convincing myself that sharing my feelings will only make things worse. I couldn't carry my family's pain. I couldn't carry my own.

At Josiah's funeral, a friend who had lost her son told me not to shut each other out of our pain, no matter what. Allowing one another into our personal anguish would help us heal together, not apart. Her words rang in my ears for many months.

One day, I got a call from Austin's girlfriend. It was late at night, and he'd made her leave our house and was talking about killing himself. I knew what an arsenal of weapons he had in his room, and I ran upstairs. I heard water running. I yelled his name and he came to the door, telling me to go away. I told him I'd stand there all night until he came out to talk to me. He got in the shower. So I sat there. Jason made his way up the stairs and sat beside me. When Austin finished his shower, he opened the door and saw us both sitting there. He completely broke down, sliding down the wall and sobbing uncontrollably.

For the next three hours, we laughed and cried and screamed, and then it hit us. We all felt the same way. We had been trying to shelter one another from the pain, and we each walked through the pain alone in the process. Our little family realized we had to take on the beast of grief together. We had to talk about it together. From that moment, we learned to reach out to each other when we felt our worst.

"Broken together" became our family's motto. Letting each other into our inner affliction proved to be a challenge, especially for Jason, who carried so much guilt and repeatedly told me he didn't want to bring me down with his soul's harassment. The night before Josiah died, Jason's very last words to him were, "Josiah, don't use drugs, son." Instead of something like, "If you feel sad or weak, it's completely normal. It's okay," or "If you feel let down by something or someone, let's talk about it," or "I bet you're feeling sad, and I want you to know I'm here to help you walk through your feelings." So many options of things to say, but we humans tend to go back to what is natural. On the other side of the spectrum, I had to learn to say things like, "Oh, you don't have a ride. What are you going to do?" when normally I'd say, "I'll take off work and take you." I often told Jason that Josiah loved him and wouldn't want him to beat himself up. But this is Jason's journey too. He has to process it without demands from me.

We both felt horrible and loved our son deeply. We would have given our lives for him. But we refused to place any shame, hatred, or blame on the other. I'd heard of marriages and families breaking apart after the death of a child, one spouse blaming the other and slinging hate words from a place of deep mourning. We wouldn't let that happen.

Incredibly, we got through the worst thing we'd ever been through and slowly learned to teach our hearts to beat again. Though it was a slow process—it continues on to this day—we are learning our new normal. A life without our Josiah is indeed a life that takes time to unlearn.

Previous things in our lives had shaped us, but nothing like the world of addiction. This world transformed who we were. We had more resolve and love, and we loved differently. What felt completely backwards, we did anyway. We learned to appreciate life and value one another. We finally realized that we could, together, overcome just about anything.

"Weeping may endure for a night
but joy comes in the morning."
— Psalms 30:5

THERE'S NO MAGIC PILL to heal grief. There are no steps or rules to follow. Everyone grieves differently. In my family, although we all felt a shared pain, we each reacted to it differently. To truly love one another, we had to understand that we were all created different and that pain looks distinct for each of us.

In pain, Jason withdrew his "normal" ways of showing love. Austin was angry and unpredictable. Montana threw herself into work and put on a tough exterior. I buried my head in church seven days a week and piled more and more onto my plate. We all handled the unhandleable differently.

We each allowed one another to do what we needed to do in order to heal and let go of what we thought the other should be or do. We were honest in our own feelings and didn't try to correct anyone else's. By loving each other right where we were, we created a safe environment in which we could heal together. We became a family who trusted each other with our worst pain. We had been shattered into a million pieces, but we began to understand that our pieces were being put back together stronger than they ever had been.

CHAPTER 14
Anchored in Hope

It was months after Josiah had died. I started having very prominent dreams. In each of them, I saw a world that appeared externally terrible. Inside, though, I was possessed by courage and strength.

Waking from the dreams, I didn't feel strong, but I could feel something happening inside of me that I couldn't explain. Things still looked and felt horrible, but I wasn't so disrupted or shaken by it anymore. My life suddenly felt like it was anchored.

Then it happened.

I had never stopped going to church for morning prayer. For months, though, I could only muster a few words. One morning as I sat in prayer, my mind conjured an image of a fire inside of me. It quickly consumed my entire being. I had no idea what it meant or what to do with it.

In the weeks to come, it became clearer. I came to understand exactly what the image was telling me. The fire was a drive birthed inside of me, a way of using my pain as rocket fuel, plunging me forward regardless of oppressive feelings. It was my courage and passion, which had been aroused in order to help other families with loved ones suffering from addiction. Much like the dog turned to ashes after sitting through the fire only to be resurrected in the master and use his voice to speak.

My fire was my burgeoning ability to view the addict as one of my own and be a voice in the midst of the devastation of addiction. The message I have to share with the world is not my message. This is God's work, and I'm the conduit, His "feet on the ground."

After Josiah died, there was this fire inside me. I wanted to gain knowledge in an attempt to educate myself and others of the horrors of addiction. To broaden my understanding, I decided to go into the state prison for interviews with addicts. One heroin addict I interviewed told me drugs were his best friend. They made him feel better than anything ever had before, numbing him to any and all of the stress life threw at him. Drugs made all his shame and pain go away. After years of "chasing the dragon," though, he was exhausted. Completely drained, he wanted to die. He had lost his job, his family, his wife, and two kids. He had stolen from anyone and everyone he could. He had lied and manipulated, cheated and hurt everyone who had ever loved him. He said the Grim Reaper had been tormenting him. He only hoped he wouldn't wake up from his next dragon ride.

Another addict told me it had all begun in good fun. The kids were all smoking pot and drinking. His father had been an addict, so he considered himself predisposed to addiction. His mom had warned him as a young kid. He recalled the year the party kids started college and the addicts started chasing the drug, their new full-time job. Drug addiction became part of his identity. When he awoke in the morning, he had a routine he was committed to for the rest of his life. As he put it, "Once you're stuck, you're stuck." We can all relate to this in one way or another. It's natural to become attached to our identities whether they be "drug addict," "mother," or "workaholic." It's a hard cycle to get unstuck from.

He overdosed on many occasions, just wanting to get high. He said no one wants to overdose, they just want to get high. He lost many friends to overdose, including his best friend who grew up in a great family and was just as addicted to heroin as he was. The loss pushed him into isolation and deeper relationship to the addiction, the friend who wouldn't die. He wondered, "Why me? Why did I make it and my friend died?" The thoughts haunted him.

There is a cold, hard truth. You and I cannot stop addiction. We can't heal our addict. But there are many things we can do to be a small part of the cure. We can break through the shame that society places on addicts and their families. We can band together in transparency and prevent others from silencing our stories. We have to be people of promise and hope. We have to be educated. We have to unlearn the judgment and shame that have kept us divided. We have to be bold and fierce in our pursuit to help fellow sufferers. We have to educate others to do the same.

Shortly after Josiah died, I was contacted by one of my close friends. He stated that the young man who sold Josiah the fatal dose of heroin was having a hard time. He was riddled with guilt and was willing to talk and tell me everything.

This young man needed me? Are you kidding me? My first thought was, "How could he ask this of me right now?" As a mom, I protect and fight for and against anything that can hurt my child. My child is now dead, and the man who gave him the fatal dose of poison needed me to help him. But after much prayer, I knew he needed to do this to be set free from it. I agreed.

The time came and I stood in a room at the church, paralyzed by fear and anxiety. I heard his mom walk in and speak to the pastor who directed them to meet me. She saw me first and wrapped her arms around me and apologized for my loss. I let go of her and went to him.

His body was warm. The very first thought I had was: "This young man has a heartbeat."

My perspective immediately changed from my hurting heart to this young man riddled with pain. I could have held him all day. He still had a life. There was still hope. A surge of empathy coursed through my veins. In that moment, all I could feel was sorrow for his heart, his broken life, his awareness that he had given his friend a lethal dose of heroin. I understood that he had the monkey on his back and hadn't yet broken loose.

I no longer had one single feeling of hurt for myself. I no longer had any lack of forgiveness. I no longer had any feelings of hate. I wanted to help this young man live. I wanted him to turn this tragedy into something that had meaning and purpose.

Through my shattered heart, there was that anchor. The word I had hidden in my heart was pouring out of my soul. I longed that this word would lift this young life out of the grips of hell.

He asked me what he could do to make it right. Go to prison? Overdose himself? He said, "Anything, tell me and I will do it."

I told him to fight for his life, beat his addiction, and then come help fight for others who are being tormented.

I have to hold on now to the belief that somehow he heard me with his heart. I have to believe that he is going to get the help he needs, and by the time he comes back to Safford, there will be a group of people who can identify with where he had been and can hold him accountable until he gets strong enough to help others.

My heart hurts now for my youngest, Austin. He is bitter and filled with rage. He is hurt with me for meeting with this young man. I know this is all a process. I don't feel like I have all the answers. All I know is that

I want no more death, no more families being ripped to shreds by heroin or any drug, no more brothers who have to somehow navigate through the pointless pain of losing their sibling.

Drugs affect every single part of a family. The statistics of families staying together through drug addiction are staggeringly low. Broken families, broken lives, shattered hearts, we can't sit by and do nothing. We have to use this tragedy and help others! We can't continue to sweep it under the rug and pretend it doesn't exist.

Is there a stigma to families torn by drugs? Yes! Should it stop us from helping? No! Should I take my pain and exact punishment or should I use it to help people like my son? Nothing about this is easy. In fact, it is very painful.

"Therefore, we who have fled to Him for refuge can have great confidence as we hold to the hope that lies before us. This hope is a strong and trustworthy anchor for our souls."
— *Hebrews* 6:18,19

WHAT IF GOD were to place a valuable gemstone in your hand and ask you to inscribe upon it a sentence that will be read on the Last Day, a display of your purest thoughts and feelings? What care and caution would you write on this gem?

My gemstone would read: You are stronger than your setbacks; like a glow stick, you sometimes have to break in order to shine. You are more than capable of taking on any obstacle you face. I'll be watching from a distance, your biggest fan and cheerleader, as you figure out life and thrive in it. Let Christ fill you with His love daily. Everything He pours into you, pour out into all, worthy and unworthy.

Be the beacon of hope in word and deed for your addict and all those you may inscribe upon.

To call love a feeling is an understatement. Feelings are fickle. Love is the strongest force on earth. My love for Josiah will never cease writing the book of his life. His pages won't stop turning. I will use my pain as fuel. All of heaven will be proud. God never wastes our pain; He gives us beauty for ashes.

Never give up on hope. Let it be an anchor to your soul through the fiercest of storms. Keep in mind that the value of an anchor only becomes apparent once you are in a storm. When the water is calm, the anchor isn't necessary. It is only once there is a need to hold on to something so as not to be lost at sea that the anchor proves its worth.

I had been in my fair share of storms. In the fiercest storm of my life, the kind that steers you miles off course, I didn't pick up my anchor and sail away. I felt the waves slamming, but I stuck it out. When the storm challenged my survival, my anchor held me steady and kept me on course. I survived the storm, firm and secure as I propelled into my future, sure of my direction. I should have been shipwrecked. Instead, I was reminded that the best is yet to come.

Our biggest hurdles become springboards to propel us into our destiny. The things we have been through weren't for nothing. We have been through things that should have taken us out, yet here we are, stronger and more resilient than ever before. Our lives have been built out of the fire that should have consumed us. The tragedies we have walked through were the precious stones we now use to construct our life, built atop the solid foundation of Christ.

We must first be transformed before we can transform others. We are here to shine the Light, to be a beacon of hope for people who are facing the storm we have faced.

About the Author

MARIA KOUTS is the mother of a victim of the growing drug epidemic. She is devoted to using her life to share the message God gave her. Through Him, she is taking her pain and turning it into something beautiful and useful. Before this mission was placed on her heart, Maria devoted her life to raising three beautiful children. Maria lives in Safford, Arizona, with her husband, Jason. She has two adult children, Montana and Austin, and granddaughter, Aurora, and bonus grandson, Orry Junior. Maria currently serves her community as an associate pastor at The River church. Learn more about Maria's mission and the documentary at carlinientertainment.com/films.

CPSIA information can be obtained
at www.ICGtesting.com
Printed in the USA
LVHW041835130621
690121LV00010B/1970

9 781734 426502